More Praise for *Conflict without Ca_____*

"*Conflict without Casualties* fills a gap by showing leaders at any level how to leverage positive conflict. Practical, insightful, challenging, relevant."
—**Dan Pink, *New York Times* bestselling author**

"*Conflict without Casualties* is powerful but in a practical way. Dr. Regier provides a compelling model to demonstrate how the energy created by conflict can be utilized for positive change—for individuals, within relationships, for organizations, and even for world crises. His analysis of the dynamics within the 'drama triangle' of persecutor-victim-rescuer clarifies most of the dysfunction seen in workplace relationships. The beauty of the concept, however, blossoms more fully as he describes the positive power created from the 'compassion cycle' of openness-resourcefulness-persistence. Thought-provoking yet easy to read and comprehend, this book is highly recommended to anyone interested in transforming the negative cycles in relationships (both work-based and personal) into the energy that will fuel positive growth."
—**Paul White, PhD, coauthor of *The 5 Languages of Appreciation in the Workplace*, *Rising above a Toxic Workplace*, and *Sync or Swim***

"We all know that drama will suck the energy out of your day, your department, and your company, but no one has identified with as much precision as Regier how to eliminate the drama and suffuse the workplace with more creativity, accountability, and productivity than ever. A revolutionary resource!"
—**Marshall Goldsmith, international bestselling author or editor of thirty-five books, including *What Got You Here Won't Get You There* and *Triggers***

"Nate Regier takes the old idea that creativity is the hidden purpose behind conflict and opposition in this world and applies it to many practical and important areas of human endeavor. His work with compassionate engagement can help sustain relationships of all kinds."
—**Michael Meade, author of *Fate and Destiny* and *Why the World Doesn't End***

"Who could ever think of conflict as creative? Nate Regier, that's who. In *Conflict without Casualties*, Nate introduces the concept of compassionate accountability—holding someone, including yourself, accountable while preserving one's dignity. His strategies are effective at work and at home—at every level. Don't shy away from conflict; face it with creativity and compassion and watch things change for the better."
—**Ken Blanchard, coauthor of *The New One Minute Manager*® and *Collaboration Begins with You***

CONFLICT
without
CASUALTIES

CONFLICT
without
CASUALTIES

A Field Guide for Leading with
Compassionate Accountability

NATE REGIER, PhD

Berrett–Koehler Publishers, Inc.
a BK Business book

Berrett-Koehler Publishers, Inc.
1333 Broadway, Suite 1000
Oakland, CA 94612-1921
Tel: (510) 817-2277   Fax: (510) 817-2278   www.bkconnection.com

Ordering Information
Quantity sales. Special discounts are available on quantity purchases by corporations,
associations, and others. For details, contact the "Special Sales Department" at the
Berrett-Koehler address above.
Individual sales. Berrett-Koehler publications are available through most bookstores.
They can also be ordered directly from Berrett-Koehler: Tel: (800) 929-2929; Fax:
(802) 864-7626; www.bkconnection.com
Orders for college textbook/course adoption use. Please contact Berrett-Koehler:
Tel: (800) 929-2929; Fax: (802) 864-7626.

Distributed to the U.S. trade and internationally by Penguin Random House Publisher Services.

Berrett-Koehler and the BK logo are registered trademarks of Berrett-Koehler Publishers, Inc.

Compassionate Accountability is a trademark of Next Element, LLC
and is currently being registered with the U.S. Patent and Trademark Office.

Printed in Canada

Berrett-Koehler books are printed on long-lasting acid-free paper. When it is available, we choose
paper that has been manufactured by environmentally responsible processes. These may include
using trees grown in sustainable forests, incorporating recycled paper, minimizing chlorine in
bleaching, or recycling the energy produced at the paper mill.

Library of Congress Cataloging-in-Publication Data

Names: Regier, Nate, author.
Title: Conflict without casualties : a field guide for leading
   with compassionate accountability / Nate Regier, Ph.D.
Description: Second edition. | Oakland : Berrett-Koehler Publishers, Inc., [2016] |
Includes bibliographical references.
Identifiers: LCCN 2016050074 | ISBN 9781523082605 (pbk.)
Subjects: LCSH: Leadership. | Conflict management. |
Responsibility. | Compassion. | Interpersonal relations.
Classification: LCC HD57.7 .R4454 2016 | DDC 658.3/145—dc23
LC record available at https://lccn.loc.gov/2016050074

Second Edition
23 22 21   10 9 8 7 6 5 4

Book producer: Westchester Publishing Services
Cover designer: Nancy Austin

To my parents, who planted and watered the seeds of compassionate accountability.

Contents

Acknowledgments

Jon Gordon is a really nice guy! I first heard him speak at the World Leaders Conference in 2015. He is an 11-time *New York Times* best-selling author, leadership coach, and motivational speaker. His message of positive energy and servant leadership resonated with me so I began following his work.

The more I worked on this book, the more I became convinced that it needed legs. It needed the best chance possible to succeed. So I reached out to Jon on the remote chance that he'd give me a few minutes to bounce around ideas, brainstorm title concepts, and lend me some of his tremendous positive energy. If you've ever taken the risk of asking for what you want, you will understand how I felt. Within a few hours I got a message back from Ann Carlson, Jon's delightful "VP of Details." By the way, that's the coolest title I've seen in a long time! Ann referred me to Jon's podcast on book publishing and offered to set up a call with him after I'd listened to the recording. I was thrilled!

I listened to Jon's podcast and it was just what I needed; inspirational, informative, and actionable. It helped me discern this one very important thing: This is the book I was meant to write, the book I want my kids to read because it is who I am and what I stand for. I passionately want to share this message and these tools with the world.

Jon took my call and it was terrific. He was supportive, affirming, helpful, and open. At the time of my call with Jon, I still didn't have a title for the book, and was anxious about it. Jon brainstormed with me and reassured me to be patient. "Don't try too hard," he said. "If you have faith it will come." And it did. Thank you Jon, for your inspiration and help. You may never know how big an impact a phone call or text can make in a person's life. It made a huge difference for me. Thank you.

Every day I am grateful for my wonderful team at Next Element. It truly is an amazing laboratory for developing, testing, and living what we teach. Every day I am challenged to live into a better version of myself. Every day I am touched by the genuine love my teammates have for each other. Every day I am amazed by their passion for making a difference in people's lives. Thank you for inspiring me, pushing me, and giving me permission to write this book!

To my mentors, I appreciate you so much! Taibi Kahler, you gave me the gift of PCM® and have been like a second father to me since my dad died. Thank you Steven Karpman for supporting our work, and for sharing your enthusiasm and endless creativity around the Drama Triangle. John Parr, your friendship, wisdom, and depth of knowledge around all things process has been such a gift.

Laurie Carney, Scott Light, and the team at Strategy Group in Wichita, KS, you are much more than a creative studio. You have been a rock of stability and optimism through this process. Thank you also for your great work on cover design and interior layout.

Thank you Marian Sandmaier, our editor. I love your perspective and the elegant care you took with this manuscript.

Innovation and discovery don't happen in a vacuum. The concepts in this book have been evolving for nearly a decade within multiple relationships worldwide. Without our clients, who have generously given their time and resources to experiment with our methods for compassionate accountability, we would have no idea whether they work. Likewise, our network of certified trainers have provided invaluable feedback and dialogue to help refine our theory and methodology.

Nowhere are the casualties of negative conflict more personal than with family. And nowhere does the power of compassionate accountability make a more profound impact. I am amazed by the daily, positive impact the concepts in this book have in my personal life. I am delighted for a family that supports me in doing what I love. My deepest gratitude goes to my unbelievable wife, Julie, and our three daughters, Asha, Emily and Lauren. Thank you for being patient with me when I stumble, for graciously letting me tell stories about you when I'm at work, and most of all, for believing in me. When life gets crazy and work seems to become too important, I remind myself of this quote from Jon Gordon, "I don't want to be a big household name. I want to be a big name in my household."

CONFLICT
without
CASUALTIES

Introduction

It was January 2012 and I was sitting on a plane with my wife, Julie, heading to Costa Rica to celebrate our 20th wedding anniversary. Little did I know that the book I was reading on the plane would help crystalize a model that my team and I at Next Element had been working on for nearly a decade. That day the seeds for this book were planted. *Conflict Without Casualties* is the manual for our guiding mission: to transform negative drama into compassionate accountability. For readers who are curious about the book that triggered my inspiration, and the process of discovering and developing the Cycle of Compassion, Chapter 5 is just for you.

I grew up the son of missionary parents in Africa. I've been asked a thousand times if I will become a missionary and if I ever want to return to Africa to follow in their footsteps. I haven't felt that calling, yet I have always believed I could be a missionary wherever I am. Guiding a company that teaches and coaches leaders to use positive conflict to create is a humbling and rewarding mission. I am grateful for this opportunity to fulfill my calling. This book is my journey and my message.

During the final stages of writing this book I struggled with how to really make this project something special. Having already written and self-published my first book, I'd already conquered my biggest fear—that nobody would care about what I wrote. A lot of people liked it. I've been blogging regularly for several years now, and that's helped me work on some other key issues: getting over worrying about other people's approval, finding my voice, and deciding what message I want to share with the world. The process of writing this book started more as a task to be accomplished, since we wanted a comprehensive reference book to support our Leading Out of Drama® training system. But the more I wrote, the more excited I became.

I believe that the misuse of conflict energy is the biggest crisis facing our world and that we haven't even begun to harness the creative potential of conflict. When people embrace the fullest meaning of compassion as a process of "struggling with" others in creative conflict, they can transform lives, companies, and the world.

In our first book, *Beyond Drama: Transcending Energy Vampires*, co-authored with my good friend and Next Element founding partner, Jeff King, we covered the key concept of Drama and Compassion at a fairly basic level. I'm so grateful for the many lives impacted by *Beyond Drama*. From Australia to Romania to Canada, our first book has helped expose the dynamics and nuances of drama and reframe the conversation around how to deal with it. *Conflict Without Casualties* represents a significant evolution of our team's thinking and practice around positive conflict.

I wrote this book because my company and I are on a mission: a mission to help people shift the balance of negative energy in the world by using conflict to create. For a decade we have successfully taught change agents such as top executives, parents, managers, teachers, and clergy to engage in conflict in a new way. We have developed a model and suite of tools to transform the energy of conflict into a creative force. These tools allow people to stop fearing conflict and start leaning into conflict for positive results.

I've always had a problem with the notion of conflict reduction, management, or mediation. All of these concepts imply that conflict is something to be lessened or eradicated, as if it's fundamentally a bad thing. I'm not surprised that many people would view conflict this way. The casualties of conflict are everywhere you look: divisive political rhetoric, religious polarization, and global ideological warfare abounds. Everywhere you look, conflict is generating casualties. Why wouldn't people want to avoid or control it?

I've seen the casualties firsthand. In high school, I lived in Botswana during the reign of apartheid in South Africa. I've witnessed police raids, murders of innocent political refugees, and car bombs that left a million pieces of flesh, metal, and clothing impaled on the thorns of an acacia tree. As a licensed clinical psychologist I've worked with victims of domestic violence who fear for their own lives and the lives of their children. I've mediated conflicts between divorcing parents and feuding executives who want nothing more than to destroy the other person's life and spirit. I've coached pastors who were pushed out of their congregations by corrupt bishops who abused their authority. I've been framed and fired from a job. I'm no stranger to destructive conflict.

Through it all, I've had the good fortune to have parents, mentors, and friends who believed there had to be a better way. They didn't reject conflict; they just knew there was a better way to use it. I listened and learned from them. I understood that eliminating the casualties of conflict cannot happen by repressing the conflict and just "being nice." It happens by stewarding the energy inherent in conflict to make something positive, even amazing. At Next Element, we've developed a method for doing this. It's called Compassionate Accountability.

You *can* engage in conflict without casualties. We have spent a decade teaching, coaching, and advising thousands of people on how to do this— refining and improving our methods over time. From Fortune 500 executives to pastors of the smallest rural churches, the concepts in this book have made a profound difference in how people walk bravely into the battlefield of conflict while preserving the dignity of all involved. If you believe that conflict can have a positive purpose, then learning how to use it well can significantly change your personal and professional relationships and the cultures in which you work.

Transformative communication involves the ability to engage in positive conflict, with compassion, to achieve results that benefit the greatest number of people. *Conflict Without Casualties* is a detailed, actionable, down-to-earth manual for how to practice compassionate accountability. If you are a change agent looking for powerful tools to leverage conflict to catalyze change, this book is for you. If you are a mediator looking for tools to break an impasse, this book is for you. If you are a manager who avoids conflict because you want to keep the peace, this book is for you. If you are a parent who has high standards for your children and can't seem to bring up the subject without alienating them, this book is for you. If you are a CEO who wants a higher level of accountability from your people while preserving their dignity, this book is for you. If you are tired of the negative drain of drama and want a set of tools for leading yourself and others out of drama, this book is for you.

Negative conflict, manifested as workplace drama, costs the U.S. economy more than $350 billion per year in the currency of broken relationships, dysfunctional teams, morale and engagement problems, and failure to thrive. Part one of this book, "Conflict With Casualties: Drama Is Killing Us," invites readers into an incisive exploration of the dynamics, motives, behaviors, costs and consequences of negative conflict through the lens of Karpman's Drama

Triangle. A day in the life of persons working at Drama Corp exposes the answers to questions like: What are the insidious ways drama manifests in the workplace? What are the basic principles of gossip? What do drama-based cultures look like? What happens when people try to help when under the influence of drama? Why do people keep acting this way when it hurts themselves and others?

A vast majority of leaders mistakenly assume conflict is the problem. They try to minimize the casualties by either avoiding conflict or controlling, mediating, or managing it. While this may reduce their stress, it also compromises the positive, creative potential in conflict. There's a better way. The second part of this book teaches readers about Next Element's proprietary model, the Compassion Cycle, a researched and tested framework for resisting the negative pull of drama, making healthier choices and using positive conflict to lead others down a better path. The Next Element team has trained thousands of leaders in these concepts and the positive results are profound. Readers will meet Juanita, the head of marketing at Compassion Corp, a leader who shows us how to apply compassionate accountability in her workplace relationships. Readers will be guided through step-by-step applications, and see multiple examples and case studies to show how the concepts can work in their lives.

The more powerful the tool, the more important the stewardship of that tool. Part three is the user's manual, the nitty-gritty rules and formulas for effectively putting compassionate accountability to work every day. This is where readers really gain confidence and understanding for how to take the concepts off the page and into their most important relationships.

Conflict Without Casualties is packed with user-friendly principles, personal stories, real-life examples and case studies, provocative questions for discussion, and easy-to-follow strategies to begin building your compassionate accountability skill set. The book is designed to be used in a variety of personal and professional growth settings. Are you working through the book on your own or with a coach? We've developed specific personal reflection and development questions at the end of the book. Would you like to use it as a book study or centerpiece of a team-development program? A companion discussion guide for just that purpose can be purchased separately. A glossary will help readers keep track of new concepts and definitions.

Any great learning quest involves a solid assessment of your current state. We've developed the *Drama Resilience Assessment (DRA™)*, an online assessment to gain insight into your drama tendencies and compassion potentials. Go to next-element.com/conflict-without-casualties to complete one free assessment and receive your results. Use these results to add context and value to your book study, team-building efforts, or coaching program. If you complete the DRA™ for individual purposes, you will only be allowed to rate yourself and receive a basic profile report. If you complete the DRA™ as part of a professional training or coaching program, you may have the opportunity to rate your team or another individual and receive a more comprehensive profile report. Do you want to measure change in your compassionate accountability? Take the DRA™ again and compare your results.

Some readers may wish for specific applications of compassionate accountability to topics like meetings, strategic planning, leading change, or supervisor-employee performance conversations. I can assure you that this book has plenty of tips you can apply in any of these situations. You won't see a chapter with any of these titles, because I've chosen to keep this book focused on the theory and methods of compassionate accountability: the essential toolkit. The principles are applicable in so many settings that it would be difficult to narrow it down to just a few.

Do you want to take your skills to the next level and become a part of our worldwide professional network? Leading Out of Drama (LOD®) is our system for comprehensive training, skill-building, and coaching for compassionate accountability. Visit our website or call Next Element to find out more about professional certification programs or to find a certified LOD® professional near you.

Enough introduction. Let's begin.

PART 1

CONFLICT WITH CASUALTIES

Drama Is Killing Us

ONE

Conflict

THE BIG BANG OF COMMUNICATION

"A problem only exists if there is a difference between what is actually happening and what you desire to be happening."

—Ken Blanchard

At the most basic level, conflict is a gap between what we want and what we are experiencing at any given moment. Conflict is everywhere. I want my latte in my hands before 7:50 a.m. so I can get to work on time, and the line is long at Starbucks. I want my team to come together around our strategic vision, and they have lot of questions. I want to feel rested tomorrow, and I also want to stay up tonight to watch three episodes of my favorite show on Netflix. I want to be recognized for my hard work on a project, and my client criticizes it. I want to feel settled about a decision, and my gut clenches whenever I think of it. I want to feel confident that my sales team will positively represent our brand in front of customers, and they question each other's integrity. I want to feel safe in my house, and I am afraid because two families in my neighborhood have been victims of recent break-ins.

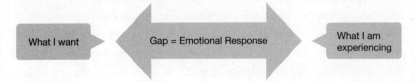

What happens when conflict occurs? Where do you feel it? Does your heart rate soar? What about your stomach? Does it churn or tighten up? Perhaps your hands get cold and clammy or your neck gets hot. Does your hair stand up on the back of your neck? Maybe you notice racing thoughts or extreme emotions. Some people shut down. Some people lash out. Some people have learned to take it in stride. But for most of us, conflict is stressful. The more conflict we experience, the bigger the emotional, physical, and psychological toll it takes on us.

CONFLICT GENERATES ENERGY

Before evaluating whether conflict is good or bad, or how we should respond to it, it's important to recognize that conflict generates energy. That energy shows up in a variety of ways. It could show up in racing thoughts and fantasies about what to do next. It could show up in increased heartbeat and flushed face caused by increased cortisol levels in the bloodstream. It could show up as an overwhelming desire to fight back or run away.

Conflict generates energy, pure and simple. And conflict is unavoidable. In fact, I'd go so far as to say that conflict is part of the grand design of the universe. I'm convinced that conflict is a necessary part of our human experience. Humans are created to be different from each other. Because of this we will inevitably have different needs, wants, and pursuits. When these come into contact with each other, conflict occurs.

Conflict is energy. Conflict is unavoidable. The only real question is: what will you do with the energy created by conflict? How *will* you spend it?

WHEN CONFLICT COMES KNOCKING, HOW DO YOU STRUGGLE?

Our experience working in thousands of interpersonal conflict situations shows that when conflict occurs, human beings struggle. We spend the energy struggling. That struggle seems to take one of two forms: we either struggle against or we struggle with.

Struggling *against* is a process of opposition and destruction. It's about taking sides, forming camps, viewing the struggle as a win-lose proposition, and adopting an adversarial attitude toward resolving the discrepancy between what we want and what we're getting. Struggling against is everywhere. It's in politics and religion. On the news. On social media. Look no further than a typical Facebook post to see self-righteous, moralistic, opinionated, and dogmatic attitudes that create and maintain polarized "us vs. them" struggles.

Struggling *with* is a process of mutuality and creation. It's about seeing the solution as a two-way street, viewing the struggle as an opportunity for a win-win outcome, and adopting an attitude of shared responsibility for resolving the discrepancy between what we want and what we are experiencing.

"The purpose of conflict is to create."

—Michael Meade

A friend of mine, the poet, psychologist, mythologist, and musician Michael Meade, says "the purpose of conflict is to create." Wow, that's a strong statement! I agree. If conflict is inevitable and it generates energy, and if creating something new requires energy, then all the pieces are in place. The determining factor is whether the energy of conflict will be used productively to create, or destructively to tear down. That choice is up to us. Each one of us has the power to transform the energy of conflict into a creative force.

This notion of conflict is quite different from what I was taught in school, and even what I see in most leadership literature. Conventional wisdom says that conflict is supposed to be managed, reduced, or controlled. Why? Because most people are accustomed to struggling *against* during conflict. When we ask people what's the first thing that comes to mind when they think of conflict, they nearly always use phrases like, "very stressful," "people get hurt," "nothing good comes out of it," "I avoid it if I can," or "I gotta win." We rarely hear an enthusiastic endorsement of conflict as a creative force. We also rarely meet a leader who has mastered the art of positive, generative conflict.

DRAMA AND COMPASSION

Two critical concepts in this book, and in our entire philosophy of transformative communication, are Drama and Compassion. You will see these themes repeated, expanded and applied throughout this book and our work at Next Element.

Drama is the result of mismanaging the energy of conflict. It diverts energy towards the pursuit of self-justification, one of the strongest human urges and one that almost always gets us into trouble.

The word compassion originates from the Latin root meaning "co-suffering." Com means "with" or "together" or "alongside." Passion means suffering or struggling. Together, these reveal a process of struggling with others.

Compassion is the result of people taking ownership of their feelings, thoughts and behaviors, and choosing to spend the energy of conflict pursuing effective solutions that preserve the dignity of all involved. Compassion is more than care and concern for others. It's about the willingness to get in the trenches and struggle together as an equal with others.

The greatest change agents in history, those who have made the biggest positive difference, have practiced this kind of compassion. From Gandhi to Mandella, Mother Theresa to Martin Luther King, each has struggled *with* instead of *against*. The next chapter unpacks the dynamics, behaviors, and consequences of drama, which is what happens when people struggle against themselves and each other.

Appendix A is a Personal Development Guide, that is geared specifically for those who would like to go deeper with the concepts from each chapter. Use this guide in your personal development, with your coach or counselor, or with a trusted friend or mentor. The guide is organized by chapter number and title so you can easily find the applicable items.

TWO

Drama

MISUSING THE ENERGY OF CONFLICT

Everyone loves stage drama that entertains and excites. Unexpected plot twists, heroes and heroines, bad guys and good guys. Alternatively, there's interpersonal drama that hollows out your stomach, makes you want to scream, and sucks the life out of you. Easy to sense and difficult to get a handle on, interpersonal drama is one of the most costly drains on relationships and productivity.

A DAY IN THE LIFE OF DRAMA CORP

Welcome to Drama Corp. It was Wednesday morning and the operations team assembled for its obligatory staff meeting. Fred, the Chief of Operations, was frustrated and critical of Sally's performance, saying things like, "You obviously don't care enough about your work." Sally looked down and said nothing, even though she had nothing to do with what had happened. Others in the room went silent and kept their heads down. Jim whispered to Sally that after the meeting he'd help her learn how to get on Fred's good side. For the rest of the meeting, everyone nodded in apparent agreement with whatever Fred said, and kept their own ideas to themselves.

After the meeting the drama continued and deepened. Brett found Sally in the break room and reassured her that it wasn't her fault. "Fred is just a jerk who has no idea what he's talking about," he scoffed. Jim stopped by Sally's desk and reminded her that he was on Fred's good side and had some advice for her. Meanwhile, Fred popped into Greta's office asking if she had noticed Sally's poor work as well. For the rest of the day, everyone from that meeting was preoccupied with what had happened, and the circle of drama grew. Lunch and break room interactions were tense. Side conversations and private text messages filled the office.

Fred spent more than an hour reviewing the employee conduct manual to see if he could write Sally up for insubordination. He just knew she was up to something bad. He wrote an email to HR asking for guidelines on documenting behavior. Sally felt angry all day, and was short-tempered with her teammates. Throughout the day she texted with several friends, including a few who didn't even work at Drama Corp, about what a jerk Fred was and how she couldn't wait to get out of there. One friend offered to check for openings at his company. Jim withdrew to his office and began plotting how to get more attention for his own projects in the next meeting.

WHAT IS DRAMA?

It's easy to identify the behaviors of drama: gossip, secrets, triangulating, retaliating, blaming, avoiding, turf wars, blowing up…the list goes on. A working definition that helps us get a handle on the concept is a bit more difficult. Here's what we've come up with:

Drama is what happens when people struggle against themselves or each other, with or without awareness, to feel justified about their negative behavior.

Drama is about struggling against. There's always a winner and a loser. The fight may be internal, between people, or involving companies and nations. Relationships in drama are usually adversarial.

Drama happens with or without awareness. How each person behaves in drama is predictable and habitual. It's highly predicted by personality and amazingly consistent from day to day. Because we tend to learn these behaviors in childhood, we've likely been practicing them our whole lives.

Feeling justified is the modus operandi in drama. If I'm in drama, my ultimate motivation is to be able to say, "See, I was right!" How much time do you spend in your head, or with your allies, rationalizing the negative things you do? Think back to a time when you made a poor decision or treated someone badly but didn't want to take responsibility for your behavior. What did you do instead? I bet you spent a lot of energy trying to justify it. It's the only way we can sleep at night! This is why drama has such a negative impact on productivity: people are spending enormous amounts of energy trying to feel justified.

Drama is all about negative attention behavior. Humans need attention. Period. If we don't get it in positive ways, we'll get it negatively. It's the next best thing, and far better than being ignored. In my first book, *Beyond Drama: Transcending Energy Vampires,*[1] I outlined the six types of positive attention and their negative attention counterparts.

Drama is fueled by myths. Dr. Taibi Kahler discovered four false beliefs that fuel distress, drama, and miscommunication.[2] He called these false beliefs Myths because they are very believable and drive our behavior, yet are literally false. The myths are:

> You can make me feel good emotionally.
> You can make me feel bad emotionally.
> I can make you feel good emotionally.
> I can make you feel bad emotionally.

We are often reminded by the therapists among us that, "Nobody can make you feel a certain way." Technically true, yet difficult to believe when drama strikes. Kahler's Myths help understand the nuances of how we stray from the basic existential position of "I'm OK. You're OK." These four myths are the driving force behind drama. Throughout this book I will show how one or more of these myths lurks behind so many of the negative behaviors and interactions that lead to destructive conflict. Recognizing and replacing these myths with the principles of compassionate accountability is unbelievably invigorating and freeing.

WHAT CAN BASKETBALL TEACH US ABOUT DRAMA?

Dr. Stephen Karpman loves sports. He is also an internationally acclaimed psychiatrist, author, therapist, and former athlete himself. As early as 1965, Karpman was doodling circles and symbols trying to figure out ways that a quarterback could outsmart the defensive halfback in football, or how offense beats defense in basketball. As the quarterback for the Delta Tau Delta fraternity football team at Duke, he would trick the defense by looking at two different receivers, then throwing to the third. Score! He also developed a matching set of fakes in basketball: a little fake, a big fake, then a third way to score. He went on to develop a sophisticated model of how games get played out in human interaction, discovering that it all comes down to triangles and roles. An offense lures a defense into expecting a certain role from the players who are interacting through triangles. Without notice, one or more of the players switch roles, leaving the defense wondering what happened.

Off the court, people do the same thing! We play one or more "expected" roles. And then, seemingly without notice, we switch, inviting confusion, frustration, guilt, and other nasty emotions that influence people to do what we want, in order to get what we want. The difference is that in real life, the switch causes a lot more problems than allowing a few points or missing a screen.

To explain what he discovered, Dr. Karpman developed the Drama Triangle, a model that describes how three different negative roles play off each other to keep us all guessing and, in the process, perpetuate unhealthy behavior. For this innovative work, he was awarded the Eric Berne Memorial Scientific Award by the International Transactional Analysis Association. One of the most elegant and practical models of how people interact in distress, the Drama Triangle has been an inspiration for our Leading Out of Drama® conflict communication methodology, as well as for our online Drama Resilience Assessment (DRA™). According to Karpman, it takes three to tango. Let's meet the three roles of drama.

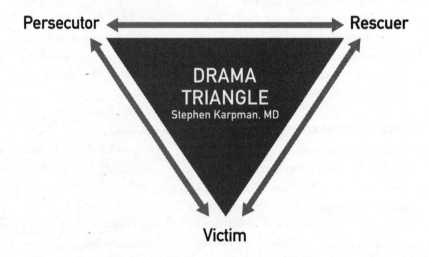

THE PERSECUTOR

At Drama Corp, Fred is the Persecutor. In drama, he resorts to criticism, questioning motives, accusations, and insults. This behavior is driven by the belief that he's OK and others are not OK, so therefore it's OK to behave this way. Whether he is aware of it or not, he has adopted the myth that he can make others feel bad to get what he wants. Fred justifies his behavior with statements like, "Sometimes you just have to show them who's boss," or "You gotta bring the hammer down or they won't respect you." Or he might declare: "They deserve it. I'm going to teach them a lesson."

Fred projects rage, arrogance, and righteous indignation to intimidate others, who most often just go along with him. Rarely does anyone confront Fred on his behavior because they are afraid of him. Even Greta, his executive peer, implicitly validates his position by agreeing or avoiding confrontation. Fred doesn't realize that he's sacrificed respect for being feared. Yet, deep down in places he doesn't want to talk about, he knows he's a tyrant. He's miserable, his family is miserable, and his people are looking for a ticket out of his department.

Fred spends a lot of energy justifying his behavior by seeking out others, like Greta, to agree with him about how worthless Sally is, or by looking to catch Sally doing something wrong in order to prove his belief that she's not OK. His self-justifying tunnel vision leads to a delusional view of reality in which people are essentially stupid, lazy and uncommitted, and will take advantage of you if you don't keep them in line. When Fred attends leadership trainings, he only "hears" things that support his view. He picks and chooses tools that perpetuate his adversarial tactics, and assiduously avoids any responsibility for his behavior.

THE VICTIM

Sally, along with several others in the Drama Corp staff meeting, play the role of Victim. In drama, Victims overadapt, surrender, lose assertiveness, accept blame for things they didn't do, and internalize the negative energy around them to avoid conflict and rejection. They are driven by the belief that others are OK, but they are not OK, therefore it's OK for people like Fred to mistreat them. Whether she's aware of it or not, Sally has adopted the myth that others can make her feel bad to coerce her into doing things, or they can make her feel good by approving of her or showing pity. She allows Brett to align with her against Fred in private because it helps her feel better but doesn't hold her accountable to do anything different. One of the most typical signs of drama is when people continually gossip and vent to feel justified, but take no responsibility for changing their behavior.

Sally justifies her behavior with Fred with statements like, "He's just trying to make me stronger" or "I probably deserved it" or "If I just do what Fred wants for long enough, eventually he will like me." She projects feelings of sadness and low self-esteem to reinforce that she's not valuable and to garner sympathy from others. These emotions also invite criticism from other Persecutors who are frustrated with her avoidance, mistakes and lack of assertiveness. This disapproval serves to further reinforce her feelings of worthlessness.

Sally doesn't realize that she's sacrificed her own self-worth in the interest of keeping the peace and avoiding conflict. Yet deep down, she is angry about how she is treated and fantasizes about one day standing up to all the Freds in her world. Meanwhile, she spends a lot of time justifying her behavior by seeking out people who tell her how badly she's being treated or give her advice that she'll never act on. Her focus on her internal struggle distracts her from the world around her and she thus sets herself up for criticism through the choices she makes, whether it means coming in late to staff meetings or spilling coffee on Fred's new shoes. Sally's self-justifying tunnel vision leads to a delusional worldview that it's her destiny to get hurt. She is convinced that if she were to stick up for herself, she would get rejected and bad things would happen.

THE RESCUER

Jim plays the role of Rescuer. In drama, he is more than willing to meddle in other people's business, show them the right way to do things, offer unsolicited advice, and push resources on them to help them be more OK. Jim is driven by the belief that he's OK and others would be more OK if they'd just let him help them, therefore it's OK to behave this way. Whether he's aware of it or not, Jim has adopted the myth that he can make others feel good by doing the thinking for them, by showing them the error of their ways and the benefits of his. He thinks he's smart to give Sally advice in private because if it goes well, he can remind her of how he saved her butt. If it goes badly, he can blame her for not doing it right. Either way, Jim "wins" and reinforces Sally's dependence on him to rescue her.

Jim justifies his behavior by telling himself, "I know what's best," or "If I don't show her how, she won't do it right," or "I'm telling her this for her own good," or "She's going to have to toughen up to make it. She should be grateful for my advice." Jim projects emotions of aloofness and arrogance to reinforce that he has it all figured out and others would be wise to recognize his intelligence and experience. His attitude and self-statements justify his need to be the savior.[3]

Jim doesn't recognize that he has invited others to sacrifice empowerment, competence and accountability, and exchange them for dependence. Deep down, he desperately wants to be genuinely connected with others and feel he's making a positive difference, yet he can't bring himself to help others develop their own autonomy because it would threaten his need to be the expert. Meanwhile, he spends a lot of energy justifying his behavior by reminding people of how terrific his solutions are, and looking for other people's problems he can fix.

Jim's self-justifying tunnel vision leads to a delusional worldview that he's been put on this earth to save others from stumbling down the wrong path.

The next table summarizes the features of the three Drama Roles illustrated in the Drama Corp scenario.

Drama Roles with Associated Beliefs, Behaviors, Justifications, Myths, and Projected Emotions

Role	Belief	Behaviors	Justification	Myth	Projected Emotions
Persecutor	I'm OK. You're not OK.	Verbally attacking others for being lazy, stupid, uncommitted, disorganized; blaming; manipulation; giving ultimatums; coercion.	Because you are the problem, it's OK for me to use fear, intimidation, and guilt to get what I want.	I can make you feel bad emotionally.	Rage, Frustration, Vengefulness, Righteous Indignation, Arrogance
Victim	I'm not OK. You're OK.	Overadapting, withdrawal, making silly mistakes, avoiding conflict, lack of assertiveness, self-doubt.	Because I am the problem, I will feel hurt because I don't deserve to be treated with dignity. I can get what I want when people pity me or try to save me.	You can make me feel good emotionally by rescuing me. or You can make me feel bad emotionally by blaming or attacking me.	Sadness, Insignificance, Fear

Role	Belief	Behaviors	Justification	Myth	Projected Emotions
Rescuer	I'm OK, you would be OK if you accepted my help and were grateful.	Meddling with unsolicited advice, withdrawing support to "toughen people up," tough love to make people better.	Because I know best, I need to help you and you would be better off if you accepted my help. I can get what I want by inviting you to let me show you how to be OK.	I can make you feel good by showing you how to be stronger and more perfect.	Superiority, Aloofness

WHAT'S IN A TRIANGLE?

Besides the fact that there are only three primary drama roles, the triangle image is critical to understanding how drama works. First of all, note that it is an equilateral triangle. All sides are of equal length, and all internal angles are the same, too. This means that each role has equal responsibility for drama. Second, the triangle is standing on its point. This illustrates how unstable the triangle is, that drama is a very volatile dynamic. Things can topple at any moment. Victim is at the bottom, representing how victims find and position themselves in the losing spot most of the time. The bi-directional arrows show that every role needs every other role in a dysfunctional, enabling way. No role can justify itself without another role to complement it. Without a Victim, the Persecutor has no one to attack. Without a Rescuer, the Victim has no one to be saved by. Without the Persecutor-Victim dynamic, the Rescuer would have no one to save.

These dynamics make the Drama Triangle very resistant to change. Because every role needs the others, and because nature hates a vacuum, every role actively recruits for other roles to fill the gap. If you've ever tried to make a major life change such as beating an addiction, leaving an abusive partner, or turning around a company culture, you have probably recognized your own drama and sought a way out. You have experienced the powerful pull of drama like a sinister vortex. You understand how hard it is to resist the invitations when everyone around you expects you to play the role you've always played so that they can keep doing what they've always done.

THE INTERNAL DRAMA TRIANGLE

Karpman's research showed that drama manifests externally through our overt behaviors, and also internally through the "voices in our head." Behind every drama role is an internal drama-triangle dialogue that supports it. The voices come from parents, significant others, teachers, and other persons whose unconditional acceptance and approval mattered to us.

Externally, Sally played a Victim role. If we could get inside Sally's head, we might hear this dialogue:

> *"You'll never amount to anything! You're just like your worthless mother!"* (Inner Persecutor)

> *"Are you going to let him talk to you like that? You're only making things worse by keeping quiet."* (Inner Rescuer)

> *"It's hopeless. No matter what I do, Fred won't like me."* (Inner Victim)

Externally, Fred played a Persecutor role. Inside Fred's head we might hear the following dialogue:

> *"You're a fraud. If the CEO knew the truth, he'd fire you in an instant!"* (Inner Persecutor)

> *"If you don't show them who's boss, they'll walk all over you."* (Inner Rescuer)

> *"Nobody respects me. I've lost control and ruined the one chance I had to gain respect from the CEO."* (Inner Victim)

Externally, Jim played the Rescuer role. What's going on behind the scenes that perpetuates his drama? He might be saying to himself:

> *"Nobody cares about your stupid advice. They just act like they are listening."* (Inner Persecutor)

> *"You better make sure Fred knows how helpful you are. That will surely get you special recognition."* (Inner Rescuer)

"I bet Fred promoted me only because I work extra hours, not because I have any real talent." (Inner Victim)

Recognizing our own internal drama dialogue can help us gain insight into how we developed these patterns in the first place, and why we act out our own external roles the way we do. Throughout this book you will be given insights and guides to better understand the dynamics and origins of your own drama triangle and what to do about it.

Knowing that behind every drama behavior is an internal drama triangle can also help us develop empathy for what other people might be going through on the inside. They are likely suffering, too.

On a beautiful spring evening in Newton, Kansas, I was on a walk with my wife and our dog. As we ambled along the country road we always walked, I heard the sound of a car behind us. I looked back and saw the most interesting thing. The car was idling along slowly with a dog trotting alongside. The dog's leash led into the car and was being held by the driver.

Immediately, I went Persecutor. "How could anyone be so lazy and unhealthy that she would drive a car to take her dog on a walk?" I asked my wife with a sneer. My wife didn't take the bait. "Maybe there's more to the story," she suggested. I didn't care and kept walking in the middle of the road, stoking my internal justification about this woman's lack of motivation and moral character.

And then she pulled up alongside us. "I feel so bad for my poor dog," she said apologetically. "I broke my foot last week and can't walk for a month. My dog and I both love our daily walks, so I figured I'd do this until I can walk again. I envy you two."

Before I verbalized anything to my wife or the kind woman, I became aware of a familiar Persecuting voice within:

"Nate, you are an ogre! This is exactly the type of insensitivity your wife is always pointing out."

"Nate, you really should withhold judgment until you learn the facts. You know what happens when you assume."

"I'm such an idiot. I bet she noticed my disdain when she drove up and knows I was judging her. As if she's not suffering enough already."

THERE'S HOPE FOR CHANGE

The number one reason people contact Next Element is because they want to reduce drama. They are tired, frustrated, confused and angry. They are trying to achieve big dreams, but people-problems keep getting in the way. Teams are fighting with each other, invisible walls go up between departments, unhealthy competition breaks out, and people stop talking to one another. Research by H2H Dynamics, a leadership training firm with expertise in human behavior, estimates that 87-percent of the workplace problems leaders face are related to people issues.[4] This is consistent with other studies showing a strong link between relationships at work and overall productivity and performance. How can an organization possibly realize its potential with so much wasteful conflict going on?

Do you personally identify with any of the drama roles? How did you feel while you were reading about Fred's, Sally's, and Jim's interactions at Drama Corp? Is your workplace a Drama Corp? How about your family, church, or sports team? What personal and professional consequences have you noticed?

The Drama Corp scenario is an everyday occurrence in most organizations. And the cost is staggering. A 2008 study on workplace conflict found that U.S. employees spent 2.8 hours per week dealing with conflict. Annually, this amounts to approximately $359 billion in paid hours (based on average hourly earnings of $17.95) or the equivalent of 385 million working days per year.[5] Add to this the psychological, physical, and emotional toll and the drag on our economy is colossal.

Thankfully, there's hope! While humans are hardwired to react with drama behavior, I doubt that most people really want to get up every day and act out their worst selves. With awareness, effort, courage, support, and practice, people, teams and whole organizations can significantly reduce drama and replace it with healthier and more productive patterns of interacting. We see these positive changes every day!

KASA Companies makes control systems for automated material-handling operations. Their clients include large automotive manufacturers such as General Motors and Toyota. Dan Stutterheim, the president of KASA, approached Next Element because he wanted to reduce drama within it's executive team. Not that people were at each other's throats, simply that the team wasn't coalescing as smoothly as Dan wanted. Their new vision was to be "a great place to work" and Dan knew it all started with their top leadership team. We embarked on a training and coaching program with the 12-member executive team to leverage their existing strengths and install more effective ways of relating and making decisions. One year later, they were communicating better, working as a team, supporting each other, addressing the real issues more openly, and spending more time focused on strategic priorities.

The most dramatic change Dan noticed was that his team spent less time in meetings. Meetings were more open, creative, and accountable than before. There was less avoiding, blaming, or talking around the issues. Dan was curious what this change was worth, so he compared time spent in meetings before their work with us, and time spent afterwards. Multiplying the saved hours by the value of those hours for each of his executive team members, he estimated $50,000 savings in one year. Add to that the ripple effect of healthier leaders, the additional impact they had by spending time with their people instead of in meetings, and the overall impact was likely many times greater than Dan's estimate.

Great leaders see drama coming a mile away and choose not to play a role in it. They develop alternative ways of influencing excellence to preserve everyone's dignity and stay focused on the most important priorities. The rest of this book is dedicated to helping you leverage positive conflict to interrupt drama in yourself, your relationships, and your organizations.

THE SILVER LINING

I believe in focusing on strengths. Playing to our strengths is a great way to gain momentum, develop confidence and maximize our potential. For some of us, those strengths are visible most of the time because we have developed the awareness and tools to avoid being triggered by external drama. For others, these strengths are intermittently available when we aren't in drama. For many, the drama has infected us for so long that we've forgotten our strengths, or they've been misused for so long that we've forgotten how it feels to shine. Really *shine*.

In our research on workplace drama, performance and personality,[6] we've discovered that behind each negative drama role are positive capacities that lay dormant or have been misused. The next three tables show these capacities:

The Positive Strengths behind Persecutor Behaviors

Negative Behavior	Latent or Misused Positive Strength
Intimidating	Dedicated
Self-Righteous	Committed
Judgmental	Conscientious
Blaming	Creative
Vengeful	Playful
Sarcastic	Spontaneous
Rigid	Responsible
Obsessive	Organized
Irrational	Logical
Manipulative	Persuasive
Jealous	Charismatic
Disingenuous	Charming
Rule-breaking	Adaptable

Let's take the skills of Organization as an example. People who are organized are a great asset in terms of their ability to synthesize ideas, keep things in order, and adhere to structure. And when they are in drama, they persecute others by becoming obsessive around order, criticizing others for being sloppy, or creating overly complex procedures that waste everyone's time. They might say, "Why can't you get it right! Don't be such an idiot."

Let's look at adaptability. We need flexible people who can respond to the unexpected and thrive under pressure. On the dark side, these same people can become Persecutors, disregarding rules and setting up negative drama so that others are caught off guard, pressuring them to adapt to the unexpected surprise. "Who needs rules," they argue. "As long as you don't get caught, it doesn't matter."

The Positive Strengths behind Rescuer Behaviors

Negative Behavior	Latent or Misused Positive Strength
Offers unsolicited advice	Dedicated
Has unrealistic expectations	Committed
Points out what's wrong	Conscientious
Invites others to question their autonomy	Persuasive
Smooth-talks to avoid negative publicity	Charming
Removes support, expecting others to toughen up	Adaptable

Here's an example: We value people who are conscientious. They are trust-worthy and we can count on them to keep our highest values in mind. And they can misuse this strength by falling into Rescuer mode, pointing out what everyone else is doing that's wrong. They convince themselves that it's noble to pursue excellence by finding and pointing out everything that's missing or broken.

Likewise, persuasive, charismatic people are a great asset because they can get people on board with any initiative. But when these same people fall into the Rescuer role, they start to persuade people to question their own autonomy and to "stick up for themselves" in a way that causes more trouble. They may say something like, "You aren't going to let Fred talk to you like that, are you?" Consider someone who is warm and caring by nature. In drama, they may play the Victim role, their warmth mutating into emotionality. If there is too much disclosure, too much sharing, and too much caring, others can feel smothered and react negatively. "I probably shouldn't share this," or "You're going to hate me for telling you this," are set-ups for rejection.

How about the spontaneous person who has the gift of being able to have fun in the moment? When playing the Victim role, they seem to lose their ability to think on their feet, as if their IQ just dropped 40 points. Have you ever seen a creative person all of a sudden start saying things like, "What? I don't get it." or, "What were we supposed to do?" Unconsciously "playing dumb" is an invitation for a Rescuer to come save them.

One of the key qualities of a good leader is the ability to solve problems without creating new ones. This is only possible when character strengths are leveraged positively, not under the influence of drama.

The Positive Strengths behind Victim Behaviors

Negative Behavior	Latent or Misused Positive Strength
Adapts too readily	Compassionate
Takes things too personally	Sensitive
Overly emotional	Warm
Can't think clearly	Spontaneous
Tries hard to understand but can't	Creative
Acts silly	Playful
Overthinks	Logical
Overworks	Responsible
Gets caught up in details	Organized
Doesn't share ideas	Reflective
Doesn't interact	Imaginative
Doesn't show emotion	Calm

One of the key qualities of a good leader is the ability to solve problems without creating new ones.

What if the energy expended in drama was redirected to leveraging the multiple strengths we have within us? How much happier would we feel? How much more productive would we be? How much less stress and illness would we suffer?

The lists of behaviors and associated strengths in this chapter can be used in a variety of ways to illuminate and predict drama, and point towards more healthy alternatives.

CULTURAL CONSEQUENCES OF DRAMA-BASED LEADERSHIP

When cultures are defined by drama, the dynamics and consequences are predictable. Over time, a culture takes on the personality of its leader(s). People are capable of playing all three roles, but often play one of them more consistently. When leaders lead from within the Drama Triangle, our research and experience have revealed the following characteristics:

Victim Leaders Breed Victim Cultures

Victim leaders avoid conflict, play it safe, second-guess themselves, and antici-
pate bad things happening. Many Victim leaders are still in their positions because others feel sorry for them or are avoiding the necessary conflict to hold them accountable. Perhaps they've achieved some level of seniority or tenure that protects them. Their environments reflect their leadership type through these symptoms:

- employees with low self-confidence
- loss of respect for the leader
- a gloom-and-doom mentality
- believing that outside forces are in control
- low morale and engagement
- apathy and indifference
- avoidance of conflict
- avoidance of initiative, playing it safe

Rescuer Leaders Breed Rescuer Cultures

Rescuer leaders are often the ones who were promoted because they were responsible and hardworking. Once in a leadership position, they never learned how to develop and empower others, instead portraying themselves as the indispensable expert who has all the answers. Their culture shows it in these ways:

- low innovation
- low initiative
- fear of failure
- analysis paralysis
- death by meetings
- death by data
- dependence on the leader
- resentment of the leader
- withholding information from the leader
- silos
- low levels of collaboration

Persecutor Leaders Breed Persecutor Cultures

Fear, guilt and intimidation have worked before, and it's intoxicating to feel the temporary rush of power. These leaders don't get honest feedback because people are afraid of them. They aren't held accountable because nobody will stand up to them. They avoid information that would question their position, power, authority, or effectiveness. And their environment shows it through:

- secrecy, hiding, and avoidance
- cutthroat competition
- fear and anxiety
- blaming, manipulating, and attacking others to avoid responsibility for negative outcomes
- increased risk of abusive behavior
- high turnover
- increased risk of lawsuits

WHICH DRAMA ROLE IS MOST HARMFUL?

Everyone likes superstar employees. Companies seek them out, give them the most attention and the best opportunities, generously reward them, and give them the benefit of the doubt when they make mistakes. This group of employees wield inordinate influence. Research from Harvard Business School[7] suggests that high performers are four times as productive as average workers, while other research shows that they may generate 80-percent of a business's profits.

Harvard researchers Dylan Minor and Michael Housman discovered another group that can have an even greater effect on organizations: toxic workers. These are talented and productive people who engage in harmful behavior. What makes these employees so damaging is their combination of high productivity and toxic behaviors. Because of this, they are not held accountable for their behavior, often with the excuse that the company needs their contribution.

Minor and Housman calculated that allowing a toxic employee to stay costs a company more than twice as much as the contribution of a star performer. Specifically, avoiding a toxic worker was worth about $12,500 in turnover costs, but even the top one-percent of superstar employees added only about $5,300 to the bottom line.

The researchers argue that the actual difference could be even bigger, if you factor in other potential costs such as litigation, fines, lower employee morale, turnover, and upset customers.

A 2012 Career Builder survey[8] found that 69-percent of employers reported that their companies have been adversely affected by a bad hire this year, with 41-percent of those businesses estimating the cost to be more than $25,000. Another 24-percent reported that a bad hire (someone with lots of drama behavior) had cost them more than $50,000.

Who is likely to be toxic? Harvard Business School's study also discovered that toxic workers were more likely to have certain personality and behavioral traits. They were overconfident, self-centered, productive, and rule-following. Interestingly, workers who said that "rules must always be followed" had a 25-percent greater chance of being terminated for actually breaking the rules. They also found that people exposed to other toxic workers on their teams had a 46-percent increased likelihood of being fired for misconduct. Toxic employees breed toxic environments.

Overconfidence, self-centeredness, and rigid rule-following are all associated with the Persecutor role in the Drama Triangle. Are Persecutor leaders the most toxic of all the drama roles? Maybe. Maybe not. What our research shows is that Persecutors are more likely to be in leadership positions because of their competitive, aggressive, and self-serving attitude. Consequently, they have more capacity to do harm.

GETTING RID OF TOXIC EMPLOYEES

One of the most difficult, and most satisfying, parts of my work is coaching a leader to exit a toxic employee. No, I don't get any pleasure from seeing an employee get fired. It's the process of getting there, and the positive consequences afterward, that are so rewarding.

Most leaders have a very difficult time firing a toxic employee, especially if they recruited, hired, or trained them. It is tough to admit your investment didn't pay off, or that you couldn't save or fix this person. Working through this is a growth opportunity in itself. The toxic employee has likely built up a cadre of followers or sympathizers who will react negatively at first. This can be frightening for a leader. Toxic employees tend to act like children and throw fits when they don't get what they want, and this can bring a lot of negative attention to a leader.

Once the noxious employee has left, though, the results are almost always better than anyone could have anticipated. The web of negativity and drama that a toxic employee has woven over time is always much larger than anyone thought. And the gratitude and positive energy that emerges once the employee is gone is more than most leaders could have dreamed of.

That's the happy ending. To undertake and plow through a process like this requires humility, courage, and faith on the part of the leader. I've seen leaders mature and grow so much through this firing process, as they faced their own demons, reorganized priorities, and rebuilt relationships that had been compromised under the influence of the toxic employee. Firing such a person may make you a few enemies, usually with other toxic, drama-filled people. It will also reward you with a ton of new, healthier and more loyal employees!

Do you have any toxic employees working for you? Have you ever let a toxic employee go? How did the process unfold? What did you discover about yourself? What were the long-term consequences? What changes did you make in your own leadership behavior as you moved through this process?

If you are struggling with cultural consequences of drama and would like to make a positive change, then read on! This book will help you with the challenging process of leading out of drama. In the next chapter, you will learn about a healthy alternative to drama and explore ways to begin redirecting that negative energy into a more fulfilling way of being, both personally and professionally.

Want to enhance your learning experience?
- If you have not already obtained your free Drama Resilience Assessment, you may do so by going to www.next-element.com/conflict-without -casualties.
- Consult the Personal Development Guide in Appendix A.

THREE

But I'm Just Trying to Help!

GOOD INTENTIONS, UNINTENDED

CONSEQUENCES

Brett, a friend of Sally's who worked in the same suite, could tell she was in a bad mood. Stepping into her small office, he asked: "What's going on?" Brett always seemed to know when drama was unfolding, even if he wasn't involved. Sally didn't feel like talking, but she shared just enough to try to satisfy Brett's curiosity so he'd leave her alone.

No luck. Brett stepped back, crossed his arms, and told Sally flatly: "What you need to do is get a lawyer and start looking for a new job. I wouldn't put up with that and neither should you." Sally bit her lip and looked at the floor. "Yeah, you're probably right," she said sheepishly. "Thanks for the advice." Sally didn't mean what she said, but hoped it would get Brett to leave. Thankfully he did, but on his way out the door he reminded her that he had a lot of experience at Drama Corp and that she should seek his advice before doing anything impulsive.

Francine couldn't help herself. Having overheard bits of the conversation, she rushed into Sally's office and blurted, "I'm so sorry that Brett was so insensitive to you. If you want me to tell him to leave you alone, I will. As for Fred, it was my fault that the report wasn't in on time. I'll go tell Fred that he should really be angry at me, not you."

Sally immediately felt defensive. "I can take care of myself, damn it!" she snapped. "Just stay out of it!" Francine retreated to her desk, apologizing profusely for making things worse.

Some people really do want to help. They have good intentions. Most of us, in fact, want to make a difference, advance noble causes, and positively influence those around us. The desire to be helpful is part of being human.

But not all helping is helpful. While under the influence of drama, people can help all they want and have the best intentions in the world, but negative consequences will result.

WHEN HELPING ISN'T HELPFUL

For the purposes of this section, let's define helping as a desire to assist another person with a task or challenge, followed by behavior intended to make a positive difference. Using this definition, only Victims and Rescuers are capable of helping. Persecutors are not. The reason is found within their myths.

Persecutors hold onto the myth, "I can make you feel bad emotionally," believing that "I'm OK. You're not OK." This pretty much eliminates them from helping. They don't want to help; they want to cause harm.

If compassion means to "struggle with," then Persecutors adopt the attitude, "I can make you struggle alone."

VICTIM HELPING

Victims hold onto the myth, "You can make me feel good (or bad) emotionally," believing, "I'm not OK. You're OK," or, in this case, "You're OK. I'd only be OK if you are pleased with my help." Because of this stance, Victims may have a noble desire to help, but only in a way that confirms their myth and false beliefs about themselves. Victim helping behavior starts with good enough intentions, but is executed with poor judgment in a way that often backfires, thus perpetuating the Victim position. Very often, their help is aimed at soothing their own need to be needed rather than real empowerment of the other person. This often appears as an anxious attempt to gain approval.

If compassion means to "struggle with," then Victims adopt the attitude, "Let me struggle instead of you."

The Victim style of helping usually sets the Victim up for criticism. Examples might include:
- Repeatedly asking, "Do you need anything?" when the other person can take care of themselves and has declined the offer more than once. At a recent family reunion, a cousin of mine kept asking if she could get me a drink, more snacks, coffee, anything. I became increasingly agitated and annoyed, thinking, "If I want something, I'll let you know! Back off!" She

made the same repeated offers to my brother, who responded by giggling and casting me a knowing glance. While neither of us said anything out loud, our body language probably sent a message of rejection.

- Offering to be a buffer, which involves talking to someone on behalf of another person, even when such an action is disastrously unwise. This is what Francine offered to do for Sally. Francine was desperate because she couldn't tolerate Sally's struggling. Wanting to make it go away, she offered to take it on by putting herself in the line of fire in order to gain approval from Sally. Bad idea.

- Independently doing something for another person, without asking them, usually without knowing all the information or context. Recently, I committed the cardinal sin for parents of athletes. I contacted my daughter's volleyball coach, unbeknownst to her, to complain about how she was being utilized on the court. The next day all the parents received an email from the coach reminding us of the policy to wait 24-hours after a match to talk to the coach. I think he was trying to tell me something!

Victim helping is targeted at Rescuers, but often ends up flushing out a Persecutor. The frequent result of Victim helping is that people don't appreciate or acknowledge the help, express resentment, or even reject the helper. This serves to perpetuate the Victim's core myths and drive them deeper into a Victim mentality. They will often interpret rejection as "See, even when I try to help I mess up." Sally rejected Francine's offer because she felt defensive and didn't want someone else to take charge of her struggle without her consent.

RESCUER HELPING

Rescuers hold onto the myth, "I can make you feel good emotionally," believing, "I'm OK. You're only OK if you let me fix you." They may desire to help, but they do it in a way that reinforces dependence (targeting a Victim) and keeps them at arm's length from the other person. A Rescuer usually starts with the good intention of protecting someone from a negative outcome. Rescuers are good at anticipating bad things that could happen and often feel confident that they have "the answer" to prevent it. However, their deeper motivation is to boost their own ego, reinforcing how smart they are, and exporting any uncomfortable feelings they have onto the other person rather than supporting that individual's capability and autonomy.

If compassion means to "struggle with," then Rescuers adopt the attitude, "You do the struggling instead of me."

Rescuer helping is usually aimed at lobbing unsolicited advice from a safe distance, while keeping an emotional arm's length to prevent intimacy and connection. Examples might include:

- Giving advice without being asked. Brett inserted himself in Sally's life without permission. Rescuers like Brett have a knack for seeing other people's problems and offering solutions with the attitude that they know best.
- Starting sentences with, "What you should do is...." or "Why don't you...."
- Suggesting action that could backfire on the other person but leaves the Rescuer out of harm's way. If Sally had taken Brett's advice, the risk to Sally would have increased with no threat to Brett.
- Assuming that because something has worked for you, it will work for someone else. Brett assumed that his experience would be helpful to Sally. I'm amazed at the cavalier attitude of smokers or drinkers who "quit cold turkey" and counsel others to do the same, assuming that anyone could easily follow their example. It's a set-up. The faulty reasoning implied by this Rescuer statement is, "If you can't do it like I did, you've got a problem."

Rescuer helping is targeted at Victims. Ideally they will take the advice, benefit from it, and show their appreciation by stroking the ego of the Rescuer. If it doesn't go well for the Victim, the Rescuer can easily switch to the Persecutor role and blame the Victim for messing it up ("That's not what I said. You did it all wrong.") or attack them for not taking the advice ("How dumb can you be? If you'd taken my advice you wouldn't be in this mess.") Either way, the Rescuer walks away unscathed, leaving the Victim to struggle alone. The Rescuer's core belief, "I'm OK. You would be OK if you followed my advice and were grateful," conveniently protects them from taking any personal responsibility for the negative impact of their helping behavior.

Drama-based helping fosters an unsavory mix of unhealthy emotions. It cultivates uncertainty, neediness, resentment, anxiety, narcissism, entitlement, dependency, and defensiveness, just to name a few. These emotions are all driven and perpetuated by the myths inherent in the Victim and Rescuer positions. Helping from either a Victim or Rescuer position results in more drama and creates more problems.

Features of Victim and Rescuer Helping

	Victim Helping	Rescuer Helping
Myth	You can make me feel good emotionally by approving of my help	I can make you feel good emotionally by giving you advice
False Belief	You're OK. I'm OK if you like my help	I'm OK. You're OK only if you let me fix you
Overall goal	Buffer someone else from negative outcomes	Demonstrate how smart and capable I am
If it turns out well	Avoid credit	Take all the credit
If it backfires	Take it personally	Blame or attack the other person
Emotional investment	High, make it too personal	Low, keep an emotional distance without support
Who struggles	I'll struggle instead of you	You'll struggle instead of me

DRAMA-BASED COACHING AND CONSULTING RELATIONSHIPS

As helpful as modern-day coaches and consultants can be, there are a lot of drama-based practitioners out there. This is what we hear from our clients who have had bad experiences in the past.

"The coach was a know-it-all. He didn't take time to understand my situation before starting to give me advice." (Rescuer helping)

"The consultant kept us guessing and didn't give us all the information. We didn't feel as though we were getting more confident in ourselves. I think she wanted us to be dependent on her." (Rescuer helping)

"The consultant did whatever we wanted. He just caved in and didn't keep us accountable. What good is that?" (Victim helping)

"If I disagreed or pushed back, the consultant would treat me like I
was ignorant and tell me to just trust him. I thought I was paying him
to help me!" (Persecutor)

If you can relate to any of these statements, you may have been in a relationship with a drama-based coach or consultant. Drama-based helping is very
common in the coaching and consulting world because it preys on fear, insecurity, and myths. Compassion-based coaching and consulting supports environments that are safe, curious, and consistent instead. Hopefully the concepts
from this book can help you avoid these types of damaging relationships in the
future, or move out of them going forward.

DRAMA ALLIES AND ADVERSARIES:
FANNING THE FLAMES OF GOSSIP

The Drama Triangle has a very well-funded recruiting
department.

Persons in drama seek out others to justify their negative behavior and perpetuate the myths associated with that behavior. I like to say that the Drama
Triangle has a very well-funded recruiting department with seemingly endless
tactics for finding others who will participate in their games.[1] Two dynamics
in particular keep the negative conflict going and divert energy away from
compassionate accountability and productive problem-solving. First, let's review
the definition of drama:

Drama is what happens when people struggle against
themselves or each other, with or without awareness, to feel
justified about their negative behavior.

People struggle against themselves or each other to feel justified about negative behavior. This happens in two ways.

Drama Allies
A Drama Ally is someone who plays the same drama role as you, which validates
and reinforces your negative behavior. These people love to join you and gang
up on a third party. Drama allies usually share a similar drama role tendency.

Victim allies offer affirmations like, "You always get picked on. I can't believe he's being so mean to you again." These affirmations invite other Victims to align with them in the false belief, "We are not OK. Others are OK." Francine attempted a Victim alliance with Sally, supporting Sally's role as a Victim and reinforcing that Fred is the Persecutor. It may seem as though Francine is playing the role of the Persecutor by calling Brett insensitive and making him out to be the bad guy. This is true at the internal level, because behind every external role is an internal drama triangle fanning the flames. Refer back to Chapter 2 for the section on the internal drama triangle.

Rescuers also form alliances. A Rescuer will recruit another Rescuer with statements like, "I know what's best for him. Don't you think I should tell him?" or "See what I mean? They'd be much better off if they'd take my advice." Ally invitations like these are recruitment efforts meant to persuade another Rescuer to validate and reinforce their false belief, "I'm OK. Others would be OK if they would take my advice and let me fix them." They are looking for a response like, "I know! They should listen to you."

Persecutors seek out other Persecutors to validate their belief, "I'm OK. You're not OK." They recruit allies with invitations like, "Teenagers are so lazy!" or "I tried to help, but they didn't take my advice. They better not come running to me to bail them out." An ally who takes the bait will respond by supporting a Persecutor's attitude with affirmations such as, "I agree. Teenagers are so self-centered, too!" or "No kidding. Maybe they will learn their lesson this time!"

Most gossip arises from people in drama who are seeking allies to validate their negative behavior.

In drama, people don't disclose their real feelings and motives, don't ask for what they want, don't attempt collaborative solutions, and don't reinforce important boundaries. They let myths drive their behavior. With or without awareness, they avoid the healthy conflict of compassionate disagreement, so they seek out others to justify their choices and behavior so they don't have to be accountable. People seeking drama allies will keep looking until they find someone to play along, moving from person to person. They will reject or avoid people who refuse to enter the drama or who directly confront it.

I was once unfriended on Facebook because I confronted a post by one of my friends that was clearly a drama-ally invitation. It wasn't surprising, I guess, because a lot of Facebook activity involves people broadcasting their drama and looking for allies. Recently, I unfriended one of my connections because I kept getting hooked by his drama-ridden posts and found myself in the throes of drama, responding in unhealthy and inappropriate ways. I didn't want to be exposed to the toxicity any longer.

What hooks you? Do you participate in gossip by forming drama alliances?

Drama Adversaries

A Drama Adversary is someone who plays a different drama role from you which validates and reinforces your negative behavior. The game is to pit two roles against each other in a way that complements and supports each role's myth. For example, if I'm playing the role of Persecutor and believe, "I can make you feel bad emotionally," then finding a Victim who believes, "You can make me feel bad emotionally," is a perfect fit! If I am Rescuer who believes, "I can make you feel good emotionally by offering you advice and saving you from your imperfections and weakness," then finding a Victim who believes, "You can make me feel good by looking out for me and telling me what's best," is a perfect fit! The purpose of drama is to reinforce myths, thus avoiding responsible accountability for behavior.

Because of how the four myths are positioned on the Drama Triangle, there are only certain adversarial combinations. Victims believe two different myths, each one abdicating the power of OK-ness to the other person. The two myths differ in terms of whether the Victim believes that someone else can make them feel good or bad. Which myth the Victim believes is influenced by how much

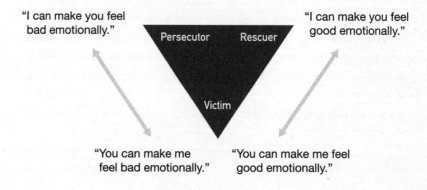

Myths Associated with the Drama Roles

"I can make you feel bad emotionally."   Persecutor   Rescuer   "I can make you feel good emotionally."

Victim

"You can make me feel bad emotionally."   "You can make me feel good emotionally."

distress they are in and who is their drama ally. If you tend toward the Victim role, you will most likely resonate with both myths depending on the situation and with whom you are relating in drama.

A Persecutor is looking only for a Victim adversary in order to validate their belief, "I'm OK. You're not OK," and their myth, "I can make you feel bad emotionally."

A Rescuer is looking only for a Victim adversary in order to validate their belief, "I'm OK. You would be OK if you'd let me fix you and appreciate my help," and their myth, "I can make you feel good emotionally by doing the thinking for you." Brett invited Sally to be his drama adversary with his unsolicited and uncaring advice to get a lawyer and start looking for another job. Sally took on the Victim role invitation by lying to Brett about her true feelings to avoid conflict.

A Victim, depending on the situation and their level of distress, may be looking for a Persecutor to validate their belief, "I'm not OK. You are OK," with the accompanying myth, "You can make me feel bad emotionally." Alternatively, a Victim may be looking for a Rescuer to validate their belief, "You're OK. I'm OK if I let you fix me," and the accompanying myth, "You can make me feel good emotionally by showing me what's best for me or approving of my help."

Here are a series of drama ally exchanges. The first statement is the invitation, the second is the acceptance of the complementary role. What roles are being played against each other in order to justify the myths?

> *"Shouldn't you call him back?"*
> *"I guess so. What would I do without you to remind me?"*

> *"What were you thinking?"*
> *"I don't know, I'm so stupid."*

> *"My email keeps locking up and I am so far behind."*
> *"You should reboot your computer."*

From the beginning, relationships with Drama Adversaries are charged with conflict. It's as if each party comes in ready for battle, expecting the exchange to turn nasty just as it has every time before. Despite the suffering that it causes, at least it's predictable. It justifies the myths and maintains the status quo.

CASE STUDY: THE PASSIVE-AGGRESSIVE CEO

Have you ever disagreed with a drama ally, or confronted them like Sally did with Francine? When you did so, what happened? Did the person retreat, or did he or she turn on you? Sometimes, people in drama who don't get the satisfaction of an alliance will switch roles and turn to adversaries instead as a way to feel justified.

Victims who don't get the satisfaction of a Rescuer feeling sorry for them and saving them may switch roles and become the Persecutor, now attacking the Rescuer for being an incompetent helper. This is one of the most toxic leadership games. I've seen it many times, and gotten burned by it at least once.

I was providing executive leadership development training for a CEO and his team. The CEO routinely played the Victim role, regularly arriving late to our training sessions, all flustered and complaining about one crisis or another. Various team members would rush to his rescue, fetching his coffee, offering to put out fires for him, and asking for extra breaks during the session so he could take care of crises.

As training progressed, the CEO's drama became more apparent to others on the team. One day during the opening check-in, a member of the executive team confronted the CEO about being late and being on his phone all the time, assertively expressing that he valued this training and wanted the CEO to be present since this was one of the agreed-upon group norms. The overall goal of my training program was to increase healthy, transparent, and assertive communication within the executive team, so I was proud of the progress reflected by this man's honest, courageous statement.

I should have anticipated what happened next.

The CEO became very defensive, switching to the Persecutor role and viciously attacking his executive for insubordination. He snapped, "How dare you question my commitment to this process? You should be grateful to have this job and to even be in this training." Then he wheeled around to face me. "Is this what you came here for, to turn my team members against me?" he spat. "It seems we've wasted our time here. Don't ask me for a reference."

The CEO pouted during the rest of that session, but had his assistant contact me afterwards to let me know that the organization would no longer be needing our services. I later learned that this CEO had a pattern of passive-aggressive manipulation, using the Victim role to garner sympathy, and then switching to the Persecutor to keep people from holding him accountable. This is a common pattern in leadership, and we've found it to be particularly prevalent in nonprofit and faith-based organizations. Why? Because passionate, committed people with big hearts are drawn to this line of work. Passion and commitment most easily morphs into Persecutor, and big-hearted love for people most easily morphs into Victim.

CASE STUDY: CRUELLA DE VIL'S FIRST DAY ON THE JOB

The Rescuer/Persecutor switch is also scary. Early on in our company's history, we fell into a hornet's nest due to our failure to recognize a dangerous Rescuer/ Persecutor dynamic. A global manufacturer of metal connectors hired us to facilitate an offsite retreat for their management team, with the goal of increasing cohesion and alignment around a new strategic plan. From our phone and in-person planning sessions, all seemed good leading up to the event, with positive energy and anticipation.

When we arrived at the event, the CEO introduced us to a new person whom we had not met during any of our pre-planning work. She was the just-hired-yesterday VP of HR and training, who, he explained, "will pick up where you leave off after this retreat. She won't play an active role, but will observe and contribute if she has something to offer."

We tried to build some rapport with the newbie, but quickly realized that we were in a volatile situation. Not only was there a built-in competitive element (outside consultant vs. new VP of HR), but nobody in the room knew who was in charge. The newly hired VP of HR, whom we nicknamed Cruella de Vil, was neck deep in a Rescuer role and in over her head from the beginning. During our morning presentations, she regularly interrupted us with unsolicited advice, disagreed with key messages we were trying to communicate, and generally seemed desperate to show everyone how smart and experienced she was. During breakout sessions she commandeered the conversation, steering it toward her agenda. Yet the more she talked, the more the group pulled away from her and looked to us for leadership of the retreat.

By noon on the first day, the retreat seemed on the edge of collapse. Recognizing that respect was slipping from her every time she opened her mouth, Cruella switched to Persecutor. During lunch she pulled the CEO aside and warned him that we were incompetent, were taking the group in the wrong direction, and should be dismissed so she could take over. The CEO didn't take the bait, but he also didn't intervene in her drama. That night, during a reception at the CEO's house, the mood was jovial and we felt very welcome by the managers who expressed their appreciation for our work.

The carnage only got worse the next day. Before we even began, Cruella was hard at work having side conversations. When we wrapped up the retreat, the managers expressed their gratitude and enthusiasm for our work and asked when they'd see us again. Cruella brooded in the back of the room.

We followed up with the company a few days later to debrief, and Cruella invited us to come in for a meeting. It was a two-hour drive from our office. When we arrived, an assistant escorted us into her office, where she was sitting behind her desk, seething with anger. She closed the door and proceeded to berate us for our incompetence for nearly 15 minutes. Here are some actual phrases she used; "All you did was undermine me," "How dare you," and "I can't believe they hired you." Then, without any further discussion, she commanded us to leave the premises. It was a long, silent ride home.

We never heard from Cruella again, but we heard she was fired a short time later. The CEO has contacted us several times since to do further work for the company. We didn't say no, but we have learned a lot about how to sniff out drama in advance to reduce these types of no-win situations. Drama-based cultures aren't interested in having their myths exposed or challenged.

We've learned a lot over the years, some of it the hard way. If you are a consultant, trainer, or other type of service provider, I bet you have plenty of your own stories about client relationships blowing up in your face because of drama.

In the next chapter we'll begin a journey into an alternative to drama, one that still requires hard work and results in far more rewarding outcomes.

Want to enhance your learning experience?
- Consult the Personal Development Guide in Appendix A, along with your Drama Resilience Assessment profile.

PART 2

A FRAMEWORK FOR POSITIVE CONFLICT

Compassionate Accountability
Can Change the World

FOUR

Compassion

NOT FOR THE FAINT OF HEART

One of Sally's good friends, Juanita, whom she considers a mentor, doesn't work at Drama Corp. Sally had included Juanita in her group text messages venting about Fred and sharing her anxiety about her job situation. Juanita didn't weigh in but did invite Sally to get together after work. Her text invitation read, "So sorry, Sally. I care about you. Want to meet for a drink later?"

Sally felt better knowing Juanita cared, and was looking forward to some time with a good friend. She was also a little apprehensive because Juanita hadn't joined in on the group texting. Sally was unsure how Juanita felt. In the past, Juanita was supportive, but didn't spend much energy listening to Sally complain. Juanita would change the subject or offer brief reassurance, but that was it. She never threw Fred under the bus, but neither did she criticize Sally for how she seemed to be such a doormat at work.

After a hug, some small talk, and placing their drink orders, Sally asked Juanita, "Can you believe how mean Fred was today?" Juanita responded, "Sally, I care about you and I can relate. I remember in my last job when my supervisor called me out in front of my team in a way that was demeaning and disrespectful. I was angry."

Sally felt understood and immediately assumed Juanita condoned her behavior. She continued, "It's not fair. No matter what I do, no matter how nice I am or how hard I work, I never get respect from Fred. If he just realized how hard I work, he'd be nicer."

Sally didn't expect what came next. Juanita leaned forward in her chair and looked Sally straight in the eyes. "I am uncomfortable with this conversation because I want you to feel empowered and confident and I want to be helpful as a friend," she said. "I am willing to support you in problem-solving how to get what you want. I'm not willing to criticize Fred or continue to hear you complain about your situation and put yourself down. I care about you."

Sally immediately noticed her heart racing and her face flushing, and didn't know what to say next. She felt embarrassed and defensive, even a little angry that Juanita didn't come to her rescue or join forces with her to criticize Fred.

Sally was experiencing something very rare in her drama-filled life. She was experiencing the conflict of compassion. Juanita's response conveyed a very different message, a message with which Sally was very uncomfortable because it contradicted all of her drama-based attitudes, beliefs, and behaviors about herself and others in her life.

Juanita's response sent three important messages of compassion:

1. You (and I) are worthwhile.
2. You (and I) are capable.
3. You (and I) are accountable.

Let's break it down by analyzing each statement in their conversation:

(Juanita) *"So sorry, Sally. I care about you. Want to meet for drinks later?"* (Juanita offers empathy that validates Sally's feelings and experience without condoning her behavior.)

(Sally) *"Can you believe how mean Fred was today?"* (Sally behaves as a Victim looking for a Drama Ally.)

(Juanita) *"Sally, I care about you and I can relate. I remember in my last job when my supervisor called me out in front of my team in a way that was demeaning and disrespectful. I was angry."* (Juanita empathizes through personal experience, reinforcing that Sally's feelings are legitimate.)

(Sally) *"It's not fair. No matter what I do, no matter how nice I am or how hard I work, I never get respect from Fred. If he just realized how hard I work, he'd be nicer."* (Victim, looking for a Rescuer or Persecutor.)

(Juanita) *"I am uncomfortable with this conversation because I want you to feel empowered and confident and I want to be helpful as a friend.* (Juanita discloses her own feelings and motives for engaging in compassionate conflict with Sally, reinforcing the message that it's OK to be vulnerable and that both of them are worthwhile.)

"I am willing to support you in problem-solving how to get what you want. (Juanita offers resources without rescuing, reinforcing Sally's capability.)

"I am not willing to criticize Fred or continue to hear you complain about your situation and put yourself down. (Juanita sets a boundary, reinforcing Sally's accountability for her behavior.)

"I care about you." (Juanita again reinforces that Sally is worthwhile.)

THE FOLLY OF ZERO-TOLERANCE POLICIES

Soon after learning about drama and identifying it in everyone else but themselves, many leaders proudly declare that they now have a "zero-tolerance policy" for drama. Some exceptionally unaware leaders even circulate our blog posts and display our No Drama stickers on their office doors to warn people that they are about to enter a "no-drama zone." Their message is that drama will no longer be tolerated, not a single solitary bit of it. Starting now.

Ah, if it were only this easy! Anyone who has read the book *Leadership and Self-Deception*[1] will recognize the folly of this behavior. The notion of zero tolerance is itself drama. It is indicative of all-or-nothing, black-or-white thinking. It reveals an overly simplistic view of conflict—that if you just don't tolerate it, it will magically disappear. One client of ours announced to her group during a training, "I divorce drama." In my experience, anyone who jumps to this conclusion is probably responsible for most of the drama on the team, but can't see it because they are too deep into their own self-justifying myths and behaviors.

The shortsightedness of zero-tolerance policies is the failure to recognize a simple fact: nature hates a vacuum.

If you remove one strategy for getting what you want, you must replace it with something else in order to be successful. Without clarity of what ELSE to do and without the support and skills to do something ELSE, we all revert to what has worked before and what we know how to do well. If I try to quit smoking, and have nothing ELSE to do with my hands, I may start chewing my nails or overdose on caffeine from the multiple cups of coffee I'm holding all day. One reason e-cigarettes work better than a nicotine patch for some people is that it gives them something to do with their hands. If I try to quit drinking to numb my feelings, and have nothing ELSE to assist me, I may begin blowing up at people or shutting down to avoid emotional pain. If I try to quit working too much, and have nothing ELSE to do with my time, I may become addicted to another activity like playing golf or watching television.

Juanita didn't stop at simply refusing to play the game. She went one step further, replacing drama with compassion and offering Sally a bridge to do the same. Juanita didn't write Sally off. Nor did she ignore or avoid her. She stayed engaged. She executed the true definition of compassion, which is to "co-suffer." She struggled *with* Sally to do something ELSE.

Compassion is not for the faint of heart. True compassion, the kind that allows conflict in order to create, is much more than empathy or caring, much more than going out of your way to help someone. Compared to compassion, drama is easy because when we resort to one of the three drama roles, we get to feel justified, keep our old habits, and foresee how things will turn out. It's predictable.

Compassion requires humility, creativity, and courage. Compassion doesn't mean letting someone off the hook, feeling sorry for them, or "loving them into good behavior."

Compassion balances caring, concern, empathy and transparency with boundaries, goals, aspirations, and standards. It's the engine that turns conflict into a creative force.

Compassionate accountability is the process of holding someone (including yourself) accountable while preserving their dignity. Compassion energizes us to co-create something amazing. Juanita set the stage with Sally. Her response sent the message that drama won't happen with her *and* that Juanita is willing to struggle with Sally toward healthier options. The problem is by no means solved, perhaps not even identified yet. But Juanita has just changed the rules of the game.

Compassion in leadership makes a real difference. Multiple studies from several major universities have found that a compassionate leader has significant positive impact on morale, engagement, and performance.[2] Compassion and curiosity increase employee loyalty and trust. Feelings of warmth and positive relationships at work have a greater impact on employee loyalty than the size of the employee's paycheck.

THE COMPASSION TRIO

Karpman first suggested an alternative to the Drama Triangle called the Compassion Triangle, with the skills of Persistence, Vulnerability, and Resourcefulness as the positive counterparts to Persecutor, Victim, and Rescuer respectively. These skills are necessary, but not sufficient, to mobilize a compassionate response to drama.

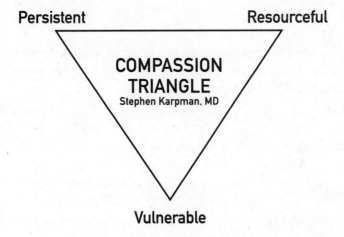

This model of compassion, which we used and taught for years, is described in detail in our first book, *Beyond Drama: Transcending Energy Vampires*, published in 2013. Since then, our thinking has evolved considerably in how we conceptualize these three skills, their relationship to each other, and their role in healthy conflict.[3] The genesis of our new model and its implications for everything from global conflict to cellular dysfunction is covered in the next chapter. For now, the most important thing is to establish and understand accurate labels and definitions.

While we loved the concept of compassion because it offered an alternative to the Drama Triangle, we weren't comfortable with the term "vulnerable." We understand the deeper meaning and positive intent of the word, and believed that in today's culture it had too many negative connotations that could get in the way with our clients. With the help of Dr. Kahler, the developer of the Process Communication Model (PCM®), we chose the word Openness to replace Vulnerability. Openness captures the essence and intent of this skill set and is more accessible to today's leaders.

Here are what we believe to be the three critical compassion competencies for negotiating creative conflict. Each competency involves three strategies, each with a specific purpose and application. Our Leading Out of Drama® model and methodologies utilize these three skills and nine strategies in many powerful ways to lean into conflict and lead out of drama.

OPENNESS

"You and I are worthwhile."

"Problems seldom exist at the level at which they are expressed. We do not see things as they are. We see things as we are."

—Anaïs Nin

Can you relate to any of the following questions?

Why won't your employees tell you what's really going on?

Why don't people follow through, even though you've been crystal clear about expectations?

Do you bend over backwards to solve customer problems and they're never satisfied?

If any of these situations ring a bell, you might benefit from increased Openness.

Openness is a state of non-judgmental receptivity to your own and others' experiences.

Openness is the healthy alternative to Victim, involving transparency, courage with self and others, self-awareness, empathy, confidence in one's own adequacy, and a willingness to own and disclose emotions. It is the key to transparency, authenticity and emotional intelligence. Openness is about being tuned in to the physical, spiritual, and psychological activity inside you, inside others, and between you and others; and accepting these with a non-judgmental attitude. Chances are, if you resonated with the negative behaviors of the Victim in the previous chapter, you are also capable of the positive alternatives listed as the counterparts to each one.

Openness is the antidote to Victim.

At its most basic level, conflict is a gap between what we want and what we are experiencing at a given point in time. Every human being wants to experience a sense of physical, psychological, and spiritual satisfaction. When we aren't experiencing it, we naturally have an emotional response. Tuning into these emotions provides rich sources of insight and guidance. The last chapter offers guidance on how to identify and use these core emotional motives to enhance your authenticity and power your positive conflict capabilities.

Develop Openness by practicing the following three core strategies. Like muscles in your body, each of these is necessary for healthy functioning, can be developed through practice, and must be used in balance for optimal functioning. Developing each of these strategies is the first skill. Learning the art of when and how to use them will come later.

THREE WAYS TO BE OPEN

Empathize

Empathy is about emotional resonance, being able to appreciate and even experience emotions from another person's perspective. Seth Godin,[4] author of 18 books on how to spread ideas, one of the world's top marketing bloggers, and a member of the Direct Marketing Association Hall of Fame, argues that good leadership requires the ability to imagine life through another's eyes.

Humans are hard-wired for empathy. Mirror neurons[5] are the brain's way of detecting and replicating another's feelings so that we can literally experience what another person is experiencing.

Empathy is more than a feeling, though. It involves understanding another's motives, emotions, and even physiological responses to a situation. Empathy allows someone to understand and anticipate how another person is experiencing (or might experience) anything from how an upcoming change initiative will affect them, to how a mentoring intervention will be received. Empathy is the key to answering the "why" behind most behavior. Empathy is how leaders show they care about others. Empathy is one of the single biggest secret ingredients in high-performing teams.[6] One of the reasons we are such fans of the Process Communication Model is because it gives insight into how different personality types perceive and experience the world, and teaches skills for decoding these perceptual frames of reference.

You may not be a natural feeler. Maybe you got a small order of mirror neurons. Still, it's possible to develop empathy by practicing some simple strategies. Over time it will come.

Tips for Practicing Empathy

- Ask questions about how a person is feeling, what's important to them, and how they are experiencing a situation. This is not about their thoughts, opinions, or strategies; it's about their emotional experiences. Examples might include, "How are you doing with this transition?" or "What concerns you the most?" or "How are you feeling today?" Avoid the most common question, "How did that make you feel?" The word "make" reinforces the myth that others are in control of our feelings. It undermines emotional intelligence and responsibility. Instead, try asking, "How do you feel about that?" or "How did you feel when that happened?"
- Affirm that it's OK to share feelings, that you care about the emotional part of another person's world. Examples; "I care about how you are feeling today. If you want to talk about it, I'd be glad to listen," or "I know this is a stressful situation, and I care about how it's affecting you."
- Take time to listen, checking your understanding by repeating back what you thought you heard until the other person is satisfied. Example: "I heard you say you're anxious about making a mistake on this project and looking silly in front of your peers. Is this accurate?" If you didn't get it

right, keep trying. It's OK to let people know that you want to understand how they are feeling and are willing to stick with it till you get it right.

- Avoid inserting your interpretations, analysis, or feelings. Empathy is *not about you.* Never say, "I know what you are feeling." People don't want you to know, they want you to care. Never start sentences with phrases like, "I think what you are feeling is…" or "Here's why you are feeling this way…"
- Relate through personal experience. This is a touchy one, because it can backfire if not done with sensitivity. The key here is to identify a time when you've had a similar feeling and share this without focusing too much on the details of the experience. An example: "I remember feeling anxious as well when we went through a restructuring at my last job." Emphasizing the shared feeling, rather than the content of the experience, prevents it from becoming competitive.

While we're on the topic of competition, keep in mind that there's a fine line between empathy and one-upping. I hate it when I disclose something important—perhaps an emotional story or experience I had—and the other person responds with a bigger, better, even more emotional story. They interrupt my mojo with something like, "I know, right? The same thing happened to me!" or "You think that's bad. Let me tell you what I went through last year."

There are two kinds of one-uppers; narcissists and good-hearted one-uppers. Narcissists can't stand not being the center of attention, so their agenda is to compete and grab the limelight. Narcissists lack empathy; they hijack emotion as a way to steal attention. Consider a conversation among a group of friends who haven't seen each other for a while. They begin to share stories of their work, vacations, and family life. One person shares about a frightening situation where they almost got hit by a car crossing a street and the group shows concern and interest. Jealous of the attention and showing no concern whatsoever, the narcissist in the group loudly interrupts with something like, "That's nothing! I was skydiving and my chute got stuck. I barely got it open in time. The instructor said he's never seen anyone so cool under pressure." The motive is to triumph over others and garner all the attention.

Good-hearted one-uppers have positive intentions, but they express it in a way that seems competitive and self-involved. In that same group of friends, let's replace the narcissist with the good-hearted one-upper. Instead of asking follow-up questions or expressing concern, she interrupts with, "I know, right? Yesterday I was walking my dog and nearly got hit by a truck." The motive is simply to get some of the attention. Sadly, good-hearted one-uppers are unaware of their behavior, and most people won't bring it to their attention. The tips above can help good-hearted one-uppers adjust their approach to be more authentic.

In contrast to one-upping are masters of empathy. They are truly moved by what others are feeling. They can relate to your experience and want you to know because they really do care. And they do it in a wonderfully affirming way that doesn't call attention to themselves.

Validate

While empathy helps us understand another's experience, validation is how we affirm that experience and a person's OK-ness as a human being. It also acknowledges that someone else's interpretation and emotional response to life is unique to them. It is neither right nor wrong, simply theirs. One of my favorite ways of appreciating emotions comes from a blog post by Josh Freedman, CEO of Six Seconds Emotional Intelligence Network. He suggests we think of emotions like waves upon the beach. Sometimes crashing, sometimes smooth, but not something to fix. They "are what they are" and they come and go in a natural flow. Feelings are real, even when the causes don't make sense to another person. And when people are struggling with difficult emotions, understanding is infinitely more precious than facts.[7] If you do a good job of validating, you can learn a lot about a person—their fears and anxieties, underlying motives, dreams and aspirations. This process can invite another person to feel extremely vulnerable and gives you a lot of power. Treat what he or she shares with extreme care. It's the abuse of closely-held feelings and motives that most damages trust.

Affirming another person's experience does not condone their behavior, nor does it mean you agree with them. It simply sends the message that the experience is real to them, and matters to you.

Tips for Practicing Validation

- Affirm the importance and impact of what the other person has shared. For example: "I can certainly appreciate how important that is for you," or "Wow, you really are excited!"
- Avoid disagreeing, discounting, or re-interpreting another person's experience through your own lens. Never say: "I don't know why you feel like that. It's not a big deal," or "What you should be feeling is…" I spent many

years invalidating the feelings of important people in my life, oblivious to how damaging it was to emotional safety and trust.

- Thank the person for letting you know how they feel. For example: "I so appreciate you sharing this with me." Or: "Thank you for sharing that. It really helps me understand what you're experiencing."

Disclose

Disclosure is about sharing how you are doing with what you are experiencing. The purpose is honesty, transparency, and rapport. What are your feelings, motives, and dreams? If they are in any way influencing your behavior, it can help to let others in on the secret. This isn't about facts and information, it's about emotions.

People often avoid disclosure because they don't trust what the other person might do with what is shared. While I can certainly appreciate this concern, I would challenge the notion that trust is about the other person's motives or behaviors. People who trust themselves are much more willing to disclose because they understand that their OK-ness is not dependent on what others think, feel, say, or do.

One of the biggest barriers to trust is a person's unwillingness to disclose the emotions driving their behavior. Here's what we hear from employees who don't trust their leaders.

"He tells me one thing, but does another."

"The council keeps asking us for reports, but never seems to be satisfied. What do they really want from us?"

"He keeps criticizing us for letting him down, but I know there's more going on. Why won't he just tell us so we can help?"

"What are they hiding?"

Very often, emotions are the real motives behind a person's behavior. Once others understand them, they can respond with a lot more empathy.

Tips for Practicing Disclosure

- Focus on your feelings. If this is difficult for you, there are plenty of self-help resources in bookstores or online to help you identify what you are feeling. I'd recommend starting with the work of Brené Brown.[8] For a start, here's a list of a few common emotions, how the body experiences them, and possible associated sensations.

Feeling	Body Location	Sensations
Sadness	Throat, Chest, Stomach	Lump, Narrowing pressure, Empty, Aching
Anger	Back of neck, Head, Shoulders, Arms, Hands	Tension, Lumps, Throbbing temples, Clenched jaw
Fear	Belly, Head, Face, Chest, Throat	Butterflies, Fluttering, Clutching, Dizziness, Shortness of breath, Tension around eyes and mouth, Dry mouth
Embarrassment	Face, Neck, Chest	Flushed and hot, Racing heart, Urge to hide
Joy	Chest, Eyes, Front of body	Glowing, Bubbly, Expansive

- Transparency feels vulnerable, especially if you aren't used to sharing feelings. Most people interpret the vulnerability as relating to the risk of what someone else might say or do with what is shared. Usually, the real problem isn't about others. It's all about how confident you are about your feelings and *your* OK-ness, and whether you know how to express feelings in healthy ways. If you struggle to express emotions in healthy ways, and/or have seen unhealthy examples of emotional expression before, you may be tentative as you gain skill in this area.
- Most people actually care and want to help. The more relevant information you give them about what's really going on with you, the more helpful they can be. For example: "I'm anxious because I really want to be done by 5 PM today. I promised my daughter I'd be at her volleyball game."
- It's OK to share a strong, negative feeling if it's motivating your behavior. As long as you own it, don't blame anyone for it, and explain why this feeling is inviting you to behave in a certain way, you have opened the

door for others to help you. An example: "What I haven't shared with you is that I care deeply about getting this promotion. As a result, I've been pushing you all pretty hard lately. That's about me, not you."

- Focus on *your* truth, not *the* truth. Disclosure is purely about you, not about what you think of others. If you are talking about anyone other than yourself, you are not being open.

RE-OFFENDING WITH MYTH-BASED EMOTIONS

As a clinical psychologist, I've spent many therapy sessions helping people to identify and express their emotions. What I've discovered is that there is a group of emotions we use every day that aren't helpful at all because they reinforce a Victim position. These emotions include:

- Rejected
- Disappointed
- Hurt
- Disrespected
- Violated
- Put-upon
- Attacked

What do these emotional labels have in common?

All of them—and many more like them—suggest that someone else did something to me, that my feeling was *caused* by someone else. This is a very common myth. People who are violated by another don't feel violated. They actually feel afraid, angry, and anxious. People who are called out in front of their peers don't feel disrespected. They most likely feel defensive, angry, or sad. Beware of emotional labels that reinforce a drama-based myth that someone else can make you feel a certain way. In drama, people don't want to learn about and take ownership over their feelings because that often requires conflict. Using myth-based emotions only perpetuate the drama.

In his book, *The Ignorant Maestro*,[9] Itay Talgam uses the analogy of a music conductor to show the power of Openness. Great conductors may know in advance how they want a piece to be played, yet they make room for the creativity and passion of their musicians. In short, they stay open. They respect the gap between the baton and instruments, appreciating that having a vision is distinct from ways of getting there. These conductors focus more on listening than on speaking and embrace their own ignorance, knowing that others may have better ideas than the conductor can imagine.

WHAT WILL YOU GAIN FROM PRACTICING OPENNESS?

- An environment of safety.
- An environment in which people are more likely to tell you what's really going on.
- Much better information to guide your problem-solving efforts.
- More trust and engagement on your team.
- A greater sense of confidence that you are dealing with the real issues.
- Increased morale.

If you want to further explore openness and dig deeper into emotional drivers of behavior, jump to the last Chapter, where I share the six core emotional motivations of conflict and illustrate how a compassionate approach can leverage these motives for positive outcomes.

RESOURCEFULNESS

"You and I are capable."

Are you a great problem-solver? Do you love a challenge? Do you get energized by figuring out the best way to accomplish a task? Do you thrive on gathering, analyzing, and curating information to reveal solutions? If so, Resourcefulness may be a strength for you. Chances are, if you resonated with the negative behaviors of the Rescuer in the previous chapter, you are also capable of the positive alternatives. Resourcefulness is the antidote to Rescuing.

Resourcefulness is the curious collection, assessment, and utilization of resources to guide action.

Resourcefulness is a brave act of curiosity and humility because it requires the abandonment of ego and judgment in favor of the most effective options and solutions, regardless of the source.[10]

If Openness reveals the real issues, motives, and emotions in our lives, then resourcefulness is the ability to problem-solve to satisfy those motives and address the issues.

When there's conflict, Openness is where we discover and affirm how the gap between what we want and what we're experiencing is affecting us. Resourcefulness is the ability to understand the gap and figure out what to do about it.

THREE WAYS TO BE RESOURCEFUL

Gather Ideas and Options

Pretty obvious, huh? Easier said than done. Gathering relevant and useful resources is much harder than we'd think. Most of us are accustomed to gathering information to support our preexisting perceptual frames of reference or stereotypes. Or maybe we only gather resources that we are aware of, neglecting other potential resources that could be helpful. Maybe we withhold resources (such as information) that would be helpful to others because we are jealous, possessive, or insecure. It's human nature to simplify our world and make it easier to understand. The challenge here is to learn as much as you can about the situation and available resources so that you can make good decisions.

Tips for Gathering Ideas and Options

- **Show a spirit of inquiry and curiosity.** Avoid sharing your ideas first, rather demonstrate your interest and receptivity to ideas and input.
- **Ask open-ended questions.** Open-ended questions invite the other person to think and give you better answers. Instead of, "Do you want to eat Italian, Mexican, or Thai?" ask, "What kind of food do you want to eat?" Instead of, "Would you rather eat first or open birthday cards?" ask, "What would you like to do first?" Some of the best open-ended questions are:
  - What options do you see?
  - How do you want to approach this?
  - What ideas do you have?
  - What resources do you have that might help?
  - What resources do you need that might help?
- **Generate lots of options.** Even if they don't seem viable, that's fine. The exercise of generating options spurs creativity. What are all the resources you can think of that might be relevant? Get them out in the open.
- **Play out scenarios.** Instead of judging an idea or option, play it out with open-ended "what if" questions. "What if we went with that option? Let's

imagine how it would go." Or, "What would happen if we did this? Why not experiment in our minds?"

- **Conduct mini-experiments.** Test ideas as rapidly and inexpensively as possible. The quicker you can do this, the quicker you'll learn what works and what doesn't.

- **Fail forward.** With experimentation comes failure. That's inevitable and OK. Failing forward means learning from our mistakes. John Maxwell's book, *Failing Forward: Turning Mistakes into Stepping Stones for Success*, is a terrific resource on this topic.[11]

- **Share the data behind your emotions and motives.** If you are upset about something that happened, describe it as objectively as possible without placing blame or making assumptions. Examples: "I saw you leaving work early on Thursday," or "I'm checking my phone to see if my daughter has had her baby yet."

- **Explain the gap.** If you've identified an emotional response to a gap between what you want and what you are experiencing, describe it simply. Examples; "I wanted to eat Mexican and all the Mexican restaurants are closed tonight," or "I was anticipating a promotion and didn't get it."

- **Disagree while respecting others' intentions and dignity.** A critical driver of innovation is the capacity to disagree, debate passionately, and explore all sides of an issue without losing respect. At Amazon, one of the company's core principles advises employees to "disagree and commit." The theory is that "harmony is often overvalued in the workplace" and "that it can stifle honest critique and encourage polite praise for flawed ideas."[12] This kind of conflict can be quite productive if done without judgement, attack or blame. It is so critical, in fact, that Patrick Lencioni, in his best-selling leadership book, *The Five Dysfunctions of a Team*, argues that this type of healthy conflict is the precursor for buy-in and results-focused teams.[13]

Build on Successes

Nothing breeds success like success. And why reinvent the wheel? Anytime you are facing a new challenge, it's helpful to explore past successes and what has worked in the past. When were you or others successful and how might the resulting learning and confidence apply now?

Tips for Building on Successes

- **Think outside the box.** Don't dismiss past successes because they don't seem to apply to the current situation. Get creative in making the connection between the past and present. Maybe you successfully dealt with a disgruntled employee in the past. You might have something to offer as you help design your organization's new customer service flow.
- **Celebrate the small things.** Break larger tasks into smaller steps. It's OK to celebrate even the smallest accomplishments. This builds confidence and momentum.
- **Set stretch goals.** Identify goals that challenge and energize a person without overwhelming and paralyzing them. You want the individual to stretch, not freeze.

Leverage Personal Strengths

The most resourceful people leverage their strengths, including past success, when they approach new problems. McGuyver, on the action TV show by the same name, was famous for his adaptability and creativity in solving problems, often with limited resources. He was able to blend his personal strengths with wisdom gleaned from past successes to come up with ingenious solutions.

During her sophomore year in high school, my oldest daughter, Lauren, went on a mission trip to Texas to help repair the home of a family whose house had been damaged by a storm. Lauren was assigned to sheetrock duty, which involved measuring and cutting sheetrock to cover walls. She had no construction experience. The project foreman working with her was extremely resourceful, probably because she'd worked with many youth who had little more than a naïve desire to help others and plenty of energy. The first thing she asked Lauren was: "What are your favorite subjects in school?" Lauren loves math; algebra and trigonometry were the ones she liked the best. "Great!" exclaimed the foreman. "Sheetrock is all about angles and measuring." She proceeded to show Lauren how to measure and reproduce dimensions from a section of wall onto a piece of sheetrock. Building on her existing strengths, Lauren quickly mastered the skill and was soon the resident sheetrock guru.

Leveraging strengths is one of best ways to boost self-confidence. Any problem can be approached by first asking, "What do I *already* know how to do that could be used in this situation?"

Tips for Leveraging Strengths

- **Explore passion and interests.** Ask yourself and others what they are good at and, equally important, what they love doing. Look beyond global statements like, "I'm a good student," and pursue more specific areas of skill and confidence by asking questions like, "What are your favorite subjects in school?"or, "What do you like most about math?"

- **Focus on strategies instead of inherent qualities.** People can't learn others' innate talent, but they can learn and practice strategies. Example of great strategies include:
  - Develop and stick to a consistent ritual before each action.
  - Generate two alternatives to each of your ideas.
  - See how well you can argue another person's position.
  - Focus on what you can control and let go of the rest.

- **Ask about, and affirm intentions.** Look for the positive intention in a person's behavior. Ask yourself, "What positive goal was he trying to accomplish?" Affirm with statements such as, "I can tell how much this means to you and how hard you are trying," or, "I am so impressed with your dedication to this cause," or, "I can see how much you care by how hard you are working to find a solution."

Strengths-based approaches are all the rage now. Everyone is focusing on strengths, based on the assumptions that you get more of what you focus on, and focusing on positives generates more engagement and positive energy than focusing on negatives. I agree for the most part. I don't want to ignore that people have weaknesses, that they often need to grow beyond their current strengths, and that sometimes our strengths aren't enough to get us from point A to point B. This is where conflict occurs. Later in this book I will directly address how to approach performance gaps and behavior problems when a person's strengths and preferences simply aren't enough to get the job done.

WHAT WILL YOU GAIN FROM PRACTICING RESOURCEFULNESS?

- An environment of curiosity.
- A more creative environment in which better solutions are discovered.
- Higher levels of innovation.
- Higher confidence and enthusiasm among employees.
- Greater levels of respect and appreciation for diversity.
- More initiative.

PERSISTENCE

"You and I are accountable."

Openness brings key emotional motives into awareness. Resourcefulness seeks to develop solutions and strategies. Persistence is all about seeing things through with integrity, humility, and respect.

Persistence is the discipline of holding self and others accountable while respecting the essential human dignity of all involved.

Persistence is more than perseverance or "stick-to-it-ive-ness." There are three key strategies of persistence, each necessary but not sufficient to combat its evil twin, Persecutor.

THREE WAYS TO BE PERSISTENT

State Your Own Boundaries and Commitments

Boundaries are non-negotiables around which you do not want to compromise. It may be a personal boundary, a deeply held conviction, or a promise you made to someone. It may be an agreement you have with another person or a contract you want to see upheld. Boundaries are not the same as ultimatums. This isn't about falling on your sword or shutting down conversation. Boundaries are the issues you are willing to struggle for. Reinforcing these non-negotiables requires a level of assertiveness that is new to most of us.

Tips for Stating Your Boundaries
- **Keep your list small and focused.** When it really comes down to it, most of us have only a few truly critical boundaries. These are the ones that cut to our soul, our sense of self, our personal and professional dignity. In our professional life, the list may be dictated by our responsibilities, commitments, and roles. In our personal life, our list might be based on personal commitments, relationships, and core values. If your list has more than six items, narrow it down. Having too many non-negotiables is a sign that you are looking for a reason to go into drama.

- **Be proactive.** It's OK to let people know of your boundaries if you antici-pate that a situation or relationship might threaten them. For example, if you are deathly allergic to nuts and your friends are planning an outing to the peanut factory, it's appropriate and important to let them know of your boundary.
- **Be explicit.** Make clear what you will and won't do, and avoid passive-aggressive ultimatums. Announcing your nut allergy is not enough. Expecting others to magically honor and accommodate your needs is irresponsible, and a setup for drama. Set explicit limits on what your behaviors will be. If your friends go, will you stay home? If so, let them know in a respectful way. Don't sulk or otherwise communicate resent-ment. If you decide to go, you might say something like, "I have a bad nut allergy. If we go to the peanut factory, I'll go take a walk, and that's fine with me."

Reinforce Non-negotiables

Everyone likes to talk about accountability; few people know how to execute it compassionately. My favorite saying is, **"Compassion without accountability gets you nowhere. Accountability without compassion gets you alienated. Blending the two is the essence of leadership."**

What does it really mean to hold someone accountable? Bringing someone to account means asking them to explain themselves or "account" for their behavior. What most supervisors and parents mean by accountability is that you can be trusted to do what you say, keep your promises, and meet your obliga-tions. It's about consistency between goals and performance, between promises and deliverables, between what you say and what you do. Accountability is commitment to walking the walk, both for you and for the other person.

Tips for Reinforcing Non-negotiables
- **Finish what you start.** Keep your promises. If you can't, or choose not to, then inform those who will be affected, discuss the situation fully and work together on what's next.
- **Own the pain and the glory.** Following through has both positive and negative ramifications. Both are yours. Don't shy away from either the pain or the glory if it's a direct result of your diligence and hard work.
- **Don't give up.** Stay the course. Do the dirty, boring, unglamorous, daily rituals that nobody notices. Angela Duckworth's research at the University

of Pennsylvania demonstrates that the key predictor of success is not talent, title, wealth, or good looks. It is grit: the ability to work hard for a long period of time toward a focused goal and keep moving forward in spite of challenges, obstacles, and failures. Duckworth says, "Grit is passion and perseverance for long-term goals. It's a marathon not a sprint."[14]

- **Remind others about commitments or goals.** It's OK to remind someone of a commitment they've made, especially if it affects you personally or if you are part of their accountability network. Examples might be, "You agreed to have the report in by Friday and it's Thursday afternoon. Will you have it in on time?" or, "We agreed that we wouldn't talk about others without them present. Will you please stop?" It might be, "Our goal is a 30-percent increase in sales. How are you doing?" or, "Our March 1 go-live date for this new medical record system is not negotiable."

- **Be straightforward about what you want.** If you want to know whether Fred will have the report in on time, ask, "Will you have the report in on time?" If your new volleyball coach has been late to practice several times and you want to know if you can count on her, ask, "Can I count on you to be on time to practice in the future?" A statement I really struggle with is, "Have you had a chance to look at the email I sent?" This statement avoids the real question, which is "Did you read the email I sent?" There's less accountability in the first statement. The second one holds the initiator accountable for asserting what they want, and holds the second party accountable for honesty about their choices. The first email attempts to lessen the chance of conflict. The second one engages the potential for conflict.

- **Use consequences carefully.** The most effective consequences have these things in common:

    a) *Naturally occurring.* Sometimes the best thing you can do is get out of the way and stop rescuing. Don't set people up to get hurt. And don't protect them and prevent them from learning how their behavior affects the world around them. Set up systems and structures so natural consequences are quick and obvious. An example might be letting an employee miss a deadline for reimbursement, whereby they don't have their money until next month. At home, I've left for work in order to be on time instead of waiting to take my daughter to school because she wasn't ready yet. She had to walk 5 blocks and barely avoided being tardy.

b) Non-emotional and non-punitive. Any consequence that secretly serves to help you feel justified or to punish another person is drama and unlikely to work well in the long run. In the examples above, the purpose was not to hurt anyone, simply to avoid rescuing and allow the natural course of events to take their toll. The key here is to avoid any follow up self-justification statements like, "See what happens?" or "Maybe you'll be ready on time tomorrow." This is drama and invites drama from the other person, thereby negating all responsibility and opportunity to make positive changes with dignity.

c) Constructive. Consequences should maximize the potential for positive learning and growth. No consequence should ever shame or humiliate another person. Persecutor leaders are infamous for calling people out in front of their peers, and scapegoating individuals with inappropriate consequences aimed at teaching everyone a lesson. Coaches who punish the whole team instead of talking to the one person who was late are engaged in destructive consequences.

Accept Responsibility and Make It Right

Accepting responsibility means owning up to your behaviors, both positive and negative. If you make a mistake, admit it and apologize. If you let someone down, acknowledge it and make it right. Taking responsibility means avoiding excuses or counterattacks, as these behaviors only serve to mask real feelings such as embarrassment, anger, fear, or loss. If you are making excuses or counterattacking, you haven't been open about, or taken ownership of, your emotional motives. In Chapter 10, I outline in detail four steps to an effective apology that combines Openness, Resourcefulness, and Persistence into a formula for genuine and impactful apologies. Here's a sneak peak. At Open the task is to disclose your feelings about what you did. At Resourceful, describe your behavior and it's consequences to show you understand what you did and how it affected people. At Persistence, say you are sorry and suggest how you will make amends or make it right. Finish at Open by listening and being receptive to how the other person responds.

Tips for Accepting Responsibility and Making It Right
- Identify the behavior in question. Don't focus on anyone else's behavior. The most important thing here is to avoid excuses, justifications, or

rationalizations for your behavior. The bottom line: what did you do and how did it affect people?

- Apologize for your behavior by saying, "I'm sorry." Don't dilute it with qualifiers like, "I'm sorry for whatever you think I did," or "I'm sorry for how you interpreted what I said." Both of these statements actually blame the other person for feeling upset.

- Offer to make it right. If you have ideas on what you could do to make amends, offer them to the other person. If not, ask them what ideas they have that would help repair the damage.

- Don't throw yourself under the bus. Just because you did a bad thing doesn't mean you are a bad person. Playing the Victim role only invites the other person into drama. Hold your head up, maintain your dignity, and show that you're capable of changing your behavior going forward.

WHAT WILL YOU GAIN FROM PRACTICING PERSISTENCE?

- An environment of consistency
- More clarity about goals and purpose
- Fewer excuses
- Better follow-through
- Improved performance
- Improved integrity and respect
- Improved reputation
- Better overall confidence in the future

DIAGNOSING JUANITA'S COMPASSIONATE RESPONSE TO SALLY

Let's revisit Juanita's response to Sally, analyzing how she used the three Compassion Skills and strategies to reinforce the three important messages of compassion.

1. You (and I) are worthwhile (Openness)
2. You (and I) are capable (Resourcefulness)
3. You (and I) are accountable (Persistence)

(Juanita) *"So sorry, Sally. I care about you. Want to meet for drinks later?"* (Openness using the strategy of validation)

(Sally) *"Can you believe how mean Fred was today?"* (Victim looking for an Ally)

(Juanita) *"Sally, I care about you and I can relate. I remember in my last job when my supervisor called me out in front of my team. I was angry."* (Openness using the strategy of empathy)

(Sally) *"It's not fair. No matter what I do, no matter how nice I am or how hard I work, I never get respect from Fred. If he just realized how hard I work, he'd be nicer."* (Victim looking for a Rescuer or Persecutor)

(Juanita) *"I am uncomfortable with this conversation because I want to be helpful and support you in feeling confident."* (Openness using strategy of disclosure)

"I am willing to support you in problem-solving how to get what you want." (Resourcefulness using the strategy of gathering ideas and options)

"I am not willing to criticize Fred or continue to hear you complain about your situation and put yourself down." (Persistence using the strategy of reinforcing a non-negotiable boundary)

"I care about you." (Openness using the strategy of validation)

Do Open, Resourceful and Persistent always work to defeat drama? Of course not. We don't even know how Sally responded to Juanita, yet. Most importantly, the three Compassion Skills and nine strategies offer a rich set of alternatives when drama comes knocking. Juanita resisted the invitations into drama while staying connected to her friend Sally. She showed the beginning of what compassion is all about, struggling WITH instead of AGAINST. She could have chosen to say many other things that would have reinforced Sally's drama-based behavior. Juanita could have gotten into her Rescuer role and said, "Unless you speak up, he'll keep mistreating you. You have to show him he can't disrespect you." She could have gone Persecutor with something like, "You're just a doormat. Everyone walks all over you."

Instead, Juanita made a different choice. It's a choice you can make as well, a choice that doesn't end up in the dead end of drama. It's a choice that can keep you engaged with people you care about while spending your energy pursuing something worthwhile.

COMPASSION SKILLS AND BALANCE

Many people ask us which compassion skill is most important, or what is the "best" score one can get on the DRA™. Neither of these questions gets to the heart of the matter. The important thing is how compassion and drama relate to one another in your life, and how your compassion skills work together in balanced harmony each day.

In later chapters, I suggest a model for how to apply each of the three compassion skills to defend against drama and engage in positive conflict. For now, let's look at the importance of balance.

Openness is necessary to support environments of safety in which we affirm our own and other people's worthiness. Resourcefulness is necessary to support environments of curiosity in which we affirm our own and other's capabilities. Persistence is necessary to support environments of consistency in which we ensure our own and others' accountability to others for our behaviors. What happens when these three skills get out of balance? Let's first look at how each skill can help us, then what happens when it is overused.

	How it helps	When it's overused
Openness	Supports emotionally safe environments Allows disclosure of the most important motives and feelings Builds connection and trust	Enmeshment and co-dependence Over-caring that leads to compassion fatigue Inappropriate disclosure and unhealthy vulnerability Poor emotional boundaries
Resourcefulness	Supports curious environments to explore options Illuminates available resources Allows creative problem-solving	Over-reliance on data as a substitute for decisions and actions False belief that enough information will eliminate all risk False belief that innovation can solve any problem

	How it helps	When it's overused
Persistence	Promotes accountability Supports environments of consistency and predictability Enables follow-through and perseverance	Rigid adherence to rules, rituals and tradition Resistance to change Dogged determination even when the plan isn't working A black-or-white, all-or-nothing mentality

As human beings, we naturally play to our strengths, favoring situations in which we're likely to be successful by doing what we're good at. But if this is all we do, over time we become a one-trick pony[15] and begin acting out the maxim, "If all you have is a hammer, the whole world is a nail." The danger in this approach is that we become increasingly out of touch with a changing world, inflexible, restricted in our range of activities, and unable to learn and grow. This is a set-up for drama, because drama is all about constraining behaviors and attitudes in order to perpetuate a distorted and stereotyped view of ourselves, each other, and the world.

People, families, organizations, and systems develop certain characteristics when their compassion skills are out of balance. As you read these lists of outcomes, consider how they fit with your own experience. Would you add, subtract, or otherwise change anything?

Low Openness, High Resourcefulness and Persistence
- High-tech, low-touch
- Performance is more important than people
- Achievement is more important than relationships
- Sales and production are more important than customer service
- Typical of many manufacturing organizations

Low Resourcefulness, High Persistence and Openness
- Tradition is more important than adapting
- People are more important than progress
- Rules are more important than innovation
- Stability is more important than change
- Typical of many nonprofit and faith-based organizations

Low Persistence, High Openness and Resourcefulness

- Initiative and fun are more important than follow-through
- Harmony is more important than accountability
- A history of abandoned initiatives
- Typical of many idealistic start-ups

The solution is to balance when and how each of these skills is applied. Doing so enables better relationships, better solutions, and better performance.

For those of you interested in how we developed our model of compassionate accountability and how it relates to the biggest and smallest problems on our planet, the next chapter is just for you. In this chapter you'll discover how the triangle became a cycle, and how human civilizations rise and fall based on their ability to negotiate certain immutable laws of compassion. It you'd like to jump straight to application and begin putting our model to work for you, skip to Part 3.

Want to enhance your learning experience?
- Consult the Personal Development Guide in Appendix A, along with your Drama Resilience Assessment profile.

FIVE

Compassion and the Cycles
of Human Civilization

WILL WE GET IT RIGHT THIS TIME?

As I mentioned in the introduction, I was on a plane with my wife, Julie, heading to Cost Rica for an early 20ᵗʰ wedding anniversary. I was reading the book, *Deep Truth: Igniting the Memory of Our Origin, History, Destiny, and Fate,* by Gregg Braden.[1] My brother introduced me to this book, and I remember being turned off by the title. I tend to reject anything that claims to be absolute. At the same time, I found the title compelling. So I began reading.

I should warn you that this chapter is simultaneously a philosophical and analytical detour from the rest of the book, and the central theoretical core of Next Element's compassionate accountability model. I debated on whether to include this chapter, make it an appendix, or cut out all the theory and philosophy and simply introduce the Cycle of Compassion as the next tool for the field guide. Eventually, I decided to keep it all in because I want readers who are curious to have the opportunity to discover the step by step evolution of this model. Also, this it the first time I've put down in writing the origins of the Cycle of Compassion and it's important to me that it is recorded.

In *Deep Truth*, Braden has attempted a paradoxical and compelling project to bring together a spiritual quest to support intelligent design with solid science on the origin and evolution of human beings. While he doesn't apologize for it, he does recognize that his approach may be difficult for persons with strong convictions in either direction.

I easily accepted many aspects of the book, disagreed with some, and was challenged by others. Overall, it captured my interest and catalyzed my conviction that compassion is at the root of how humans relate to themselves, each other, and the world around them. Here are the themes I connected with most.

We have been around longer than we think.

Our greatest strength is also our biggest liability.

Civilizations seem to rise and fall according to a predictable, cyclical pattern of behavior that reveals itself at all levels of existence.

We've been through this before. Maybe we can learn something.

WE ARE OLDER THAN WE THINK AND WE'VE BEEN HERE BEFORE

Archeological evidence shows that advanced human civilizations grew and flourished on the earth long before the traditionally accepted date of 5,000 to 5,500 years ago.

Braden shares and interprets a host of scientific evidence to support the following:

Traditional thinking about our past	Revised thinking about our past
1. Civilization has evolved one time in human history.	1. Civilization has developed multiple times in human history.
2. Civilization has developed in a linear way from less to more evolved.	2. Civilization has developed in a cyclical way, with each cycle generally developing from being less to more evolved.
3. The history of world civilizations is about 5,000 years old.	3. The most recent cycle of civilizations is 5,000 years long.
4. The oldest civilization in the world is Sumer, dating back to about 3,500 B.C.E.	4. The oldest known civilization in the world is Göbekli Tepe, now dated at 9,500 B.C.E.
5. We are living in the most advanced civilization in the history of the world.	5. Civilizations in the past were capable of technological achievements that cannot be duplicated today.

From *Deep Truth*, p. 132.

Braden argues that advanced human civilization might have existed during the end of the most recent Ice Age, approximately 12,000 years ago. He suggests two premises:

1. We've been in this world much longer than our traditional history acknowledges.
2. Something happened to our world in the past, something that brought an end to all that our ancestors had built and cherished. From the

Biblical flood to the native wisdom traditions to the Epic of Gilgamesh and the Mahabharata, we have stories to remind us of the rise and fall of civilizations.

Most intriguing for me is the notion that multiple civilizations have come and gone on this earth, each following a similar pattern of rise and fall. I wondered whether somewhere in this process we might find wisdom that could guide us toward a better future.

THE ABILITY TO ADAPT VS. THE DESIRE FOR STABILITY

In Braden's description of the common pattern of each civilization's development, there seemed to be three basic stages. First is a stage of profound vulnerability, in which the external environment dictates experience. Safety and survival are the only priorities. Proponents of evolution might argue that it is during this stage that most natural selection takes place, since those most endowed with survival traits will live to procreate. This stage lasts about 1,000–1,500 years.

Inevitably, human curiosity and ingenuity begin to emerge. The second stage is one of exploration and creativity. In this stage, people begin to learn about their world, understand how it works, and interact with it. This stage sees the creation of tools, shelter, agriculture, and domesticated livestock. These innovations allow humans to move beyond mere survival and achieve a rudimentary level of comfort and predictability. This stage most likely marks the transition from a hunter-gatherer lifestyle to the formation of communities, villages, and cities. This is the first time in the development of a civilization that humans are able to buffer themselves from the environment. Tools, shelter, machines, clothing, and other technologies significantly reduce people's vulnerability to the environment as well as their need to adapt to changing climate conditions. This enhanced safety and consistency leads to predictable patterns and the emergence of a status quo, an enduring state of conditions and values. The second stage can last between 1,500–2,000 years.

The third stage is maintenance of the status quo. Humans like comfort and predictability. Not only do these make life physically less demanding, but they also free up mental energy for higher-level pursuits such as education, written communication, philosophy, art, organized religion, and hobbies. Humans at this stage of development are motivated to protect what they have and maintain the status quo. This ensures a measure of safety, stability in food, energy, and water supplies, and allows for accumulation of wealth. Strong ideologies develop that support and perpetuate the status quo. These ideologies achieve a life of their own.

Walls, borders, laws, treaties, pacts, and organized religions are all the result of civilizations' attempts to maintain the status quo—to keep things going as they are without too many casualties. The third stage is shorter than the previous two, lasting anywhere from 250–1,000 years. This is where things begin to fall apart for humans. Braden identifies a crisis point at which any civilization inevitably arrives, characterized by these features:

1. An unsustainable population.
2. Climate change.
3. Growing shortages of fresh water and food.
4. Growing gaps between poverty and wealth, health and disease, education and illiteracy.
5. Growing threat of war and other violent conflict.

These perils are inevitable results of the three stages of civilization. Staying in one place, developing steady food and water supplies, and improving technology invariably reduces death rates but also create gaps in health and wealth status. Economies of trade, entrepreneurship, and industry make it possible for a few people to control a majority of resources and accumulate wealth. Societies seeking order and stability will value education. Because of gaps in wealth and access to resources, there will also be gaps in education and literacy since education and healthcare cost money. A growing population and increasing use of technology demands more food, more water, and more energy to sustain itself.

Climate change, whether part of naturally-occurring environmental cycles or influenced by human behavior, further threatens predictable access to food, water, and energy supplies. When these shortages occur, groups of people naturally look beyond their walls and borders for more food, water, and energy. If their quest interferes with another group's supply, conflict is inevitable because there is now competition for valuable resources among groups who are invested in maintaining their status quo. This increases the threat of war or other violent conflict. Humans are highly invested in protecting what they've worked so hard to build.

CRISIS POINTS ARE SIGNALED BY THREE TYPES OF CONFLICT

Intrapersonal Conflict

This is conflict within an individual between a desire to be independent and individually successful versus the need to coexist in community and share limited resources. Individuals also experience conflict between the body's natural tendencies toward homeostasis and unhealthy behaviors regarding food consumption, a sedentary lifestyle, and chronic stress. Currently, lifestyle-related health conditions account for the majority of healthcare expenses in the United States. These conflicts threaten the stability of the human body and psyche.

Interpersonal Conflict

The gaps of wealth, education, and access to resources cause conflict between individuals. Many revolutions are caused by an unsustainable gap between the wealthy ruling class who has control of resources, and the majority of the population upon whose backs the rich few can exist. These conflicts threaten the stability of relationships.

Regional and Geopolitical Conflict

This is the conflict caused by competition for resources between entire countries or regions. Competing ideologies are often intertwined with competition for resources. Modern-day terrorism can be seen as an ideological clash around the use and distribution of resources and moral ideologies. These conflicts threaten the safety of humanity as well as the planet itself.

What happens next? According to Braden's research, all previous civilizations have reached this crisis point and continued to fight to maintain the status quo, resulting in their own extinction. The stories that explain these extinctions are varied, but usually involve a natural disaster (environmental cause) or a human disaster (war). Either way, humans have participated in their own demise by failing to respond to a changing world, or killing each other in a desperate effort to maintain the status quo.

Today, three common storylines reflect paradoxical awareness of a crisis without awareness that we've created the problem and are participating in our own demise by doing more of the same but expecting different results. Have you heard these storylines from leaders? Politicians? The media?

We need to protect our *way of life* that we've worked so hard to create.

We need to defend our *way of life* from those who would seek to destroy it.

We need to ensure sustainable access to the resources that enable *our way of life*.

THE COMPASSION CYCLE EMERGES

You've probably already made some of the connections that crystalized for me on the flight to Costa Rica. In a matter of minutes, here's what came together in my head:

1. Humans are uniquely endowed with the ability to be open, resourceful and persistent.
2. These gifts parallel the three stages of how civilizations develop.
3. It's a process that seems to start at Open, move to Resourceful, and finally to Persistence (O-R-P).
4. When conducted in the right way, this process contributes to a constructive and creative evolutionary process. When done in the wrong way, it results in negative conflict, violence, and destruction.
5. The O-R-P process is represented at both the micro and macro levels of human existence.[2]

At this point, I realized that the Compassion Triangle is not a triangle. It is a cycle. The skills of O, R and P are not independent constructs, but three interdependent ways of feeling, thinking, and acting that work productively together.[3] The Compassion Trio is a basic value system with patterns of behavior for how people relate to themselves, each other, and the world in healthy ways.

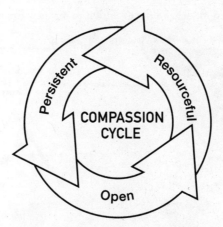

This realization raised several other questions for me. If compassion behaviors can be understood as a cycle, is there an order? A direction? A starting point? A stopping point? These questions made for spirited debate among our team! After much experimentation and discussion, we determined that the Cycle starts at Open, then Resourceful, and then to Persistent. That's what we humans have done as long as we've been around.

If this is so, why the wars, violence and conflict? Why so many casualties? Why do we keep repeating the same destructive behaviors over and over? What would happen if we went in another direction? Is there a glitch in the Force, Luke Skywalker? To answer these questions, we applied two "what if" thought experiments, which led to the discovery of the Compassion Cycle, the engine behind Next Element's Leading Out of Drama® system.

What if the cycle is meant to be continuous?

What if the O-R-P cycle actually operates within the Drama Triangle?

Here is the old model and the evolution to our new thesis.

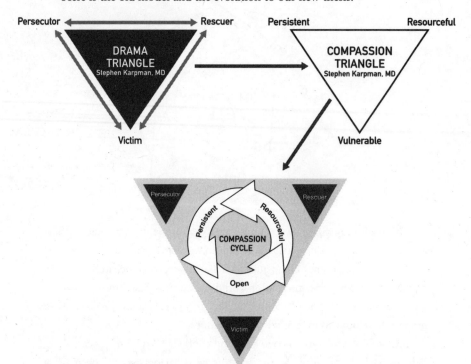

Much like looking through a different lens changes how we see the world, this new way of connecting compassion skills and drama roles opened up a flood of new possibilities. In the years that followed, our team, inspired by numerous conversations with our clients and trainers, made several significant discoveries:

Cycles imply continuous movement, while triangles imply corners and blockages.

Drama inevitably pushes us into corners, where we cling to distorted world-views that compel us to do the same thing over and over, expecting different results. Compassion, on the other hand, keeps us moving, searching, nimble, effective, and capable of adapting to change.

Movement in a circle generates centrifugal force, and it takes effort to stay on track.

Holding on to a rapidly spinning merry-go-round is hard. The faster it goes, the harder it is to stay on it. This is because of Newton's First Law of Motion: Every object in a state of uniform motion tends to remain in that state of motion unless an external force is applied to it. This is the same as Galileo's Law of Inertia. Simply stated, objects in motion want to keep going in the same direction. This gives new meaning to the definition of compassion, to "struggle with." It takes awareness, discipline, and hard work to stay on the Compassion Cycle, especially when drama invitations beckon from the dark corners of the triangle with every turn we make.

Without exerting effort to hold on and "go with" the circular motion of the cycle, humans easily slip off and fall into drama. Placing the cycle within the triangle provides a simple visual to demonstrate this human tendency. For example, when engaging Resourcefulness, if someone is moving too fast, doesn't exercise intentionality and self-control, or overdoes it, it's easy to slip into Rescuing. People who are highly resourceful are at high risk for rescuing behavior. The same is true for Openness and Persistence, the other two Compassion Skills.

Getting on the Compassion Cycle, and staying on it, is the key to resilience in the face of drama. Most of this book is dedicated to helping you do just that.

Each Compassion Skill has a natural drama counterpart.
Like two sides of a coin, Openness and Victim are inextricably intertwined. This tension is part of the human condition. Recognizing and respecting the relationship between them is critical for changing how we respond to the pull of drama. Later in the book, I will offer you practical tools to manage the dance between drama and compassion in your life.

Blocking movement along the cycle has predictable negative consequences.
Nature seems to follow the Compassion Cycle, never stopping too long at one spot, always struggling to survive, creatively seeking stability, developing habits and routines, then breaking down, re-calibrating, and starting over. Most cyclical change models propose a similar pattern, suggesting that over time the repetition of these cycles generates higher and higher levels of sophistication and adaptation.[4] Taking up residence at one place for too long results in stagnation, failure to adapt, and an increasing risk of extinction. This extinction occurs in relationships, organizations, and entire civilizations.

Humans seem to be the only species that doesn't play by the rules.
This is where we discovered the glitch. Human history is marked by a progression from Openness to Resourcefulness to Persistence, followed by a remarkable divergence in trajectory. As a species, human beings seem to have a very difficult time returning to Openness in order to keep the cycle going. We take up residence at Persistence, which inevitably morphs into Persecutor as we fight to protect what we've built and save ourselves from the consequences of our own creation. The Law of Inertia wins. In getting stuck there, we fail to adapt to a changing world and changing environment. We become so confident in our ability to solve problems and so attached to our way of life that we begin to act as though the natural order doesn't apply to us. Most major world religions might interpret this behavior by saying that humans begin to believe they are the Creator instead of the created.

Braden reminds us that no civilization to date has managed to resist the inertia that attends Persistence, extricate themselves from the Persecutor role, and get back on track to Openness. And, as history demonstrates, the farther off track we get, the harder we fall. There comes a point where course corrections are no longer an option, where the tipping point has come and gone and we doom ourselves to extinction.

WILL WE GET IT RIGHT THIS TIME?
Braden's big question, to which I've dedicated my life, is: Can we get it right this time, before it's too late?

I get up every day, enthusiastically pursuing answers to this question because I firmly believe that we *can* get it right. The Compassion Cycle not only affirms the positive potential in human beings, but also reveals a roadmap for recognizing where we are and what to do next. Although this model was inspired by the study of entire civilizations, it illuminates deep patterns of human functioning at the most intimate level. It shows us why we do what we do, and how we can bring a new level of awareness and intentionality to every single interaction.

It starts inside of each of us, then between us and others, and finally in how we come together as nations to solve the biggest problems facing our civilization.

Since that flight to Costa Rica in 2012, my team at Next Element, along with friends and colleagues around the world, has continued to explore, test, and refine our model. People of all ages, in all sorts of positions, across the globe, have used this model to transform their lives and the lives of those around them by repurposing the negative energy of drama into positive conflict. Conflict without casualties is becoming a reality around the world!

Reading *Deep Truth* was an act of Openness for me. Developing the Compassion Cycle was an act of Resourcefulness. Writing this book is a monumental effort in Persistence. And I'm brought back to Openness in every relationship with each person who interacts with our ideas, tries them on, shares their perspective, and offers improvements. The cycle continues, and it's working. The deep truth I've discovered is that compassion can change the world. In fact, it might be the only thing that will keep us alive.

Are you ready to get out of the clouds and back into real-life drama challenges? Turn the page, your compassionate accountability field guide is waiting!

Want to enhance your learning experience?
- Consult the Personal Development Guide in Appendix A, along with your Drama Resilience Assessment profile.

PART 3

CONFLICT WITHOUT CASUALTIES USER MANUAL

Putting Next Element's
Compassion Cycle to Work

SIX

Violators Will Be Prosecuted

THREE RULES OF THE COMPASSION CYCLE

Let's rejoin Sally and her friend Juanita at the coffee shop. Sally's heart is racing, her face is flushed, she feels embarrassed and defensive, and even a little angry that Juanita didn't come to her rescue or join forces with her to criticize her boss, Fred.

What caused Sally's distress? Numerous factors can be boiled down to a couple of key elements: Juanita did not validate Sally's myths, refused to play a drama role, and responded with compassionate accountability instead. Let's replay what Juanita said that precipitated Sally's discomfort.

> *"I am uncomfortable with this conversation because I want to be helpful and support you in feeling confident. I am willing to support you in problem-solving how to get what you want. I am not willing to criticize Fred or continue to hear you complain about your situation and put yourself down. I care about you."*

Juanita did something profound here. She complied with all three rules of the Compassion Cycle. Yes, the Cycle has rules. Just like our physical world has laws, the world of positive conflict has laws as well. Since discovering the Compassion Cycle, we've been experimenting and researching the inescapable rules that govern its operation. These rules are discoveries, not inventions. Gravity was not an invention; it was a discovery. It always existed, and Sir Isaac Newton figured out how to describe it, predict it, and measure it. He discovered the Law of Gravity.

Likewise, once we discovered the Compassion Cycle, we uncovered three rules that, when followed, lead to positive outcomes during conflict. When violated, predictable negative consequences occur. Once you learn about these three rules, if you're still not convinced, try ignoring them and see what happens. I tried ignoring the law of gravity many times when I was younger. It didn't turn out well.

Before launching into the rules, let's review the purpose of the Compassion Cycle. What's it for and why do we use it?

The Compassion Cycle is a philosophy, model, framework, and set of strategies for engaging any of these situations:

- When drama is occurring and you want to intervene positively
- When addressing a gap between what you want and what you are experiencing
- When you want to avoid Rescuer or Victim-helping
- When you recognize drama in yourself and want to get out
- When conflict is necessary to address behavior or performance

Let's assume you encounter one of these situations and want to apply the Compassion Cycle. Follow these three rules.

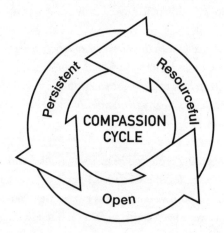

RULE 1: START AT OPEN

Kansas in spring can be one of the most beautiful places on earth. It was early on a Friday and my schedule was open. I decided to take off and start my weekend early! One of my favorite things to do is go on walks with my wife,

Julie. I didn't use to like walking. I preferred tennis to get exercise because at least I could keep score and win once in a while. Walking seemed so boring. But over time, I've come to love walking, especially with Julie. It's one part of the day we give each other our full attention and are able to talk about the most important things in our lives. We've walked together for 25 years.

What better way to kick off the weekend than a walk with Julie on a gorgeous Kansas spring afternoon? At the time, Julie was working across the street from my office as the membership coordinator for our local chamber of commerce. Her schedule was pretty flexible, so I was hopeful she could get off early and join me.

> I texted Julie: "When are you getting off work?"
> Here's what I got back: "Why?"

Not what I expected—and not what I wanted. My enthusiasm about a walk with Julie was quickly replaced with mild frustration and annoyance. "Just answer my question!" I thought. I didn't text her back right away. I needed to calm down.

Once I had gathered myself, I responded, "It's beautiful out! I'd love to go for a walk before the kids get out of school."

> Within seconds: "Sweet! I'll see if I can get off early."

During our walk I asked Julie about her response to my initial text. Why hadn't she just answered my question, and what was going through her mind at that time? She explained that when she read my question, a ton more questions flashed through her mind. "What did I forget? Was I supposed to pick up one of our girls from school early? What does he want from me?" Once I disclosed my motives it all made sense and she could answer the question. Until then, she found herself second-guessing, making assumptions, and jumping to conclusions.

I made the mistake that thousands of spouses and bosses and friends make every day. I entered at Resourceful. My question was innocent enough. I just wanted information. However, without first disclosing my feelings and motives, Julie experienced my question as loaded and maybe even a trap. Had I entered at Open first, all the drama could have been avoided. Unfortunately, when spouses, bosses, and friends conceal their real feelings and agendas, they keep the people most connected to them guessing.

Whether you are responding to negative conflict or initiating positive conflict, Openness is the most effective place to start. We've tested multiple other models of conflict and mediation that offer different options, and we've tested what happens when people start at Resourcefulness or Persistence. We are confident that Openness is the best first step.

Why?

- Openness supports an environment of emotional, physical and psychological safety that allows people to engage more fully and candidly.
- Openness reduces defensiveness in self and others, increasing the chance of collaboration.
- Openness reveals true motives and demonstrates transparency and honesty, making it possible to problem-solve the real issues up front.
- Openness affirms the value of each person involved, increasing the likelihood of win-win, lasting solutions.
- Openness engages empathy, a critical part of problem-solving difficult situations.

Openness is the least likely place a person will start during conflict. It is human nature to fight or flee when feeling threatened. The last thing I want to do is share my real motives or have empathy for you! Not only does that feel unsafe, but it ruins the whole game of drama.

Entering at Open is a tremendous act of vulnerability. It's the kind that tests your courage about whether your feelings, needs, and wants are legitimate and worthy. It's the kind that relies completely on your sense of self-worth because you can't predict whether the other person will accept or validate what you've shared. It's the kind of vulnerability you feel when you've played all your cards and don't know what's in the other person's hand.

I personally struggle to follow this rule. I break it regularly. Many times I am simply out of touch with my feelings and don't even identify that they are causing my discomfort. Sometimes I don't like to feel vulnerable or transparent because I've convinced myself it's a sign of weakness. "You can't be weak during conflict," I tell myself. "You'll lose." And then there's my ego. I know I should start with Openness, but I don't want to. I don't want to show my cards because I want to feel in control of the situation, relationship, or interaction. I don't want to struggle with anyone. I want them to struggle alone, damn it!

Rescuers struggle to enter at Open because they want to be the bullet-proof savior while the other person is the vulnerable damsel in distress. Openness evens the playing field and Rescuers don't like this. Persecutors haven't a clue how to be Open because they are so focused on why they are right and everyone else is wrong. They can't conceive of entertaining a view other than their own. They dare not stop long enough to experience their own feelings because it would be too uncomfortable. It would make them vulnerable, which to Persecutors is the scariest thing imaginable.

Victims struggle to enter at Open because they don't believe they are worth it. Openness affirms the value of all involved, including me. If I believe that I'm not OK, then why be Open? Why share real wants and feelings? They'll inevitably get smashed and I'll be rejected, so what's the point?

What if I enter somewhere other than Open? Entering at Resourceful or Persistent doesn't engender drama, so what's the problem? Sometimes this doesn't lead to conflict. I may simply ask a person what time it is (Resourceful) and they give me an answer without any drama. Other times, the problem starts small and escalates into drama over time if we repeatedly engage from a different place than Open. This is particularly true in the charged situations described earlier in this chapter. Here's what we have found as the typical consequences of entering somewhere other than Open. For the sake of this thought-exercise, let's imagine one of two potential scenarios. Either you see a person struggling and think you could help (Resourceful). Or, you want to confront a person about behavior you don't like (Conflict).

Scenario 1: One day after I arrived at work, I discovered my cell phone battery was dead. Apparently it had not charged properly the night before. I became anxious and upset about not being able to check my voicemail or send texts. I shared my anxiety and complaints with my team. One of my team members immediately started asking me questions about what charging cords I was using and offered her charging station as an option (Enter at Resourceful). I felt a surge of defensiveness and annoyance. The other team member said the following, "Oh man, that sucks. I'm sorry. And I know you are expecting an important call" (Enter at Open). I wanted to give him a hug!

An old saying came to mind: "I don't care how much you know until I know how much you care."

You see a person struggling and want to help. Entering at Resourceful—as the first team member did—is tempting. You have ideas about how you can help and want to share them. You may even have a great solution that you know would solve the problem. Maybe you are just curious and want to figure out what's going on so you can be more helpful. Chances are you will approach the distressed person by either asking a question about what's going on, or offering your perspective and knowledge on the situation.

The problem isn't with your intentions. The problem is that you have failed to acknowledge the emotional motives behind this interaction. You haven't acknowledged the suffering of the other person. And you haven't acknowledged or disclosed your own motive for engaging with them in the first place. You've ignored the heart of the person. You have not been Open.

Recognizing and affirming our own and another's emotional experience is absolutely critical before we can effectively problem-solve. The person who is struggling rarely can think clearly or be Open to your help if they don't first sense that you understand or care about their struggle. Likewise, why should they let you into their world if you haven't been honest with them about the emotions that motivated you to engage with them? Entering at Open before moving to Resourceful enables much more effective and productive interactions.

The same principle applies to conflict interactions. Before you start conflict with yourself or someone else, no matter how noble your intentions, starting at Open accomplishes the vital goal of affirming the human emotion behind the difference of opinion, thereby affirming the person.

Scenario 2: Let's imagine that one of my colleagues entered at Persistent in response to my cell phone worries. I might have heard something like, "You promised to call the client back this morning. Better find another option," or "Our policy states that the company won't pay for replacement power cords if the damage happened at home." Thankfully, I didn't hear this. I might have lost it entirely. Entering at Persistent is tempting for people who focus on rules, boundaries, promises, guidelines, and policies. Whenever there is struggle or conflict, their first question is, "What are we *supposed* to do in this situation?"

Have you ever had an experience in which a child, spouse, employee or friend comes to you in an emotionally vulnerable or volatile state, either because of something they've done or something they've experienced? Maybe your son ran out of gas on the way to work. Maybe your employee just got off the phone with an irate client. How does it go when you launch right in by reminding them of the rules, consequences, guidelines, or policies?

It's not that the rules aren't important or that promises shouldn't be kept. It's that until the emotional issue is addressed, people can't think clearly or engage effectively around problem-solving (Resourceful) or accountability (Persistence). Until we know we are worthwhile and understood, we can't engage in being capable or accountable. Openness is the prerequisite for Resourcefulness and Persistence.

Openness during conflict is instantly disarming and sometimes scary. It is like a reset button that immediately changes the rules of the game. I learned to use Openness in my therapy practice, as a powerful tool to deal with transference. Paying attention to my own feelings and bodily sensations, and sharing these appropriately with my patients, was extremely effective. If I found myself in the Rescuer position, trying desperately to fix my patient by giving them advice even in the face of obvious resistance, I would step back and reflect on my own experience. Usually, something like this would emerge: "I am feeling tense and anxious because I keep trying to give you advice that doesn't seem helpful to you. I wonder what that means."

Juanita took that risk with Sally. She confronted Sally's drama invitation with the following statement:

> *"I am uncomfortable with this conversation because I want be helpful and support you in feeling confident."*

This act of Openness demonstrated Juanita's emotional self-awareness, her courage to refuse the drama invitation, and a willingness to be vulnerable as she disclosed her real motives. She did all of this while affirming that she had no intention of engaging in a competitive interaction. Juanita conveyed the strong message that "I'm OK. You're OK. I'm not OK with the behavior." This message is powerful because it separates behavior from who the person really is and counters the myth that anyone can make anyone else feel good or bad.

Juanita put herself out there. Sally could have easily rejected any part of this statement by saying something like:

> *"I didn't mean to make you feel uncomfortable. I shouldn't have brought it up."*

> *"If you want me to feel empowered then support me, damn it."*

"You're no help. You obviously don't care."

All of these statements are drama invitations and reject Juanita's invitation for Sally to engage instead in a compassionate interaction. If Sally had responded in one of the above ways, Juanita would have been faced with a new question and choices. The first and most important is, "Am I still OK even though Sally rejected what I said?" Depending on Juanita's resilience and self-confidence, she could stay Open and remember that how someone responds to her does not define her. Or she could slip into any one of the drama roles—Victim, Rescuer, or Persecutor—and relapse into myth-based behavior.

Have you ever entered at Open only to get shot down? What happened next? Have you ever showed empathy, transparency, and vulnerability with someone in drama and nothing changed? I have. Thankfully, we discovered two more rules.

RULE 2: MOVEMENT IS NECESSARY

Each compassion skill is necessary, and not sufficient, for optimal performance. No single skill can operate in a vacuum, and no one skill is sufficient for healthy functioning. So, ya gotta keep movin'.

Movement is necessary because:

Openness only gets us so far. Openness creates safe, transparent conditions to problem-solve conflict. But it doesn't engage in problem-solving, so unless we move to Resourcefulness, the underlying issues never get addressed.

Resourcefulness only gets us so far. Resourcefulness gets us to a place of understanding and generates options. It takes us right up to the point of making a choice among options, then implementing that course of action. Unless we move to Persistence, nothing ever gets done.

Persistence only gets us so far. Persistence gets us through implementation. Now that we've actively solved the problem, we need to evaluate how it's working. Unless we move back to Openness, we can't gain the perspective necessary to fully evaluate the impact of our actions on ourselves and others, and make necessary corrections.

And the Cycle continues.

Because Openness-Resourcefulness-Persistence operates as a cycle, the Law of Inertia applies. Movement in a circular motion creates centrifugal force. This inevitably creates tension. There's tension between where I'm headed and where

I need to go, where my natural tendencies would take me and where I could better direct my energies. There is tension between what I am comfortable with and what I need to learn.

This tension, in turn, creates conflict. If I am at Open and you are at Resourceful, we have conflict of interests and motives. If I am at Persistence and need to move back to Open, there's a conflict between where I am and where I need to be. If our strategic project team is at Persistent (ready to implement a new plan) but the organization is at Open (unsure about what's going on), there is conflict.

Juanita didn't stop at Open. She kept moving, and by doing so, the tension increased, as did the conflict. Juanita recognized that all three compassion skills were necessary to mount an effective defense against Sally's drama and keep herself out of drama at the same time. She not only covered all her bases, but also complied with the rule of movement. She effectively erected barriers to drama at all three danger points, sending a clear message to Sally about the rules of engagement. It's no wonder Sally's heart rate increased! Stringing together a series of compassion statements like this is impressive! Easier said than done, yet something that all of us can learn with practice.

The first two rules tell us where to start and remind us that conflict is a natural and appropriate consequence of movement. The third rule governs order.

RULE 3: THE ONLY WAY FORWARD IS FORWARD

The Compassion Cycle moves in a counter-clockwise direction, from Openness to Resourcefulness to Persistence and back to Openness. The best results are obtained by following this order. We've tested it successfully in thousands of scenario experiments and real-life situations.

Openness creates safe, transparent conditions to problem-solve conflict. Resourcefulness picks it up from there and gets us to a place of understanding and options. Persistence takes us through implementation and completion. A return to Openness gives us the perspective necessary to fully evaluate the impact of our actions on ourselves and others. Resourcefulness makes necessary corrections which are implemented at Persistence. And so on.

Juanita did a wonderful job of moving through the cycle without staying or skipping.

What Juanita said	The Compassion Cycle rule
"I am uncomfortable with this conversation because I want be helpful and support you in feeling confident."	Enter at Open
"I am willing to support you in problem-solving how to get what you want."	Movement is Necessary (she went to Resourceful) The only way forward is forward
"I am not willing to criticize Fred or continue to hear you complain about your situation and put yourself down."	Movement is Necessary (she went to Persistence) The only way forward is forward
"I care about you."	Movement is Necessary (she returned to Open) The only way forward is forward

It's tempting to violate this rule—Movement is Necessary—by skipping the next compassion skill on the cycle. We may be weak in that skill, or perhaps we are moving too quickly and lose focus. Or it could be that the other person is really resisting. Regardless, skipping a skill causes predictable problems. Let's look at a few examples.

During strategic planning, the group has reviewed the findings of three separate consultants and constructed a pros/cons list to help them. Unable to make a decision, they form a focus group to discuss their feelings.

In this situation, the group does not move from Resourcefulness to Persistence. They fail to make a decision and implement a recommendation. The consequence is that they accomplish nothing. By going backward to Open, they hope for some sort of magical solution that will relieve them of the require-ment to engage Persistence. Many organizations fall into this trap, particularly start-ups with high levels of innovation and creativity. They are strong on Open and Resourceful, weak on Persistence. They have great ideas and few results to show for it. They find themselves awash in unfinished projects and unfulfilled dreams.

The boss has been adamant and consistent with her employees about the importance of being on time. Although she mentions it at every meeting, nothing seems to be changing. Employees wander into the office late, and few come to meetings on time. Her next strategy is to get creative and slip reminders into the employees' paycheck envelopes.

Here, the boss starts from Persistent, skips Open and plunges into Resourceful. Her plan is unlikely to be effective because she doesn't know what's really doing on. Unless she goes through Open, she won't be able to learn what is causing her employees' resistance. Because she's increasingly out of touch with them, her creative solutions at Resourceful will be limited by incomplete information.

I have an SUV that gets 12 miles per gallon when I drive it to and from work. It's a 1.5 mile commute each way. It takes me four minutes to drive, 10 minutes to bike, and 25 minutes to walk. When gas prices reached $4 per gallon several years ago I was unhappy and uncomfortable. I was spending $80 to fill my tank! So I got a bit more interested in fracking (a process of releasing natural gas from rock), the Keystone pipeline debate, and the potential for tapping into huge Alaskan oil reserves. How dare any country threaten our access to global oil reserves!

My father had many wise sayings. One of them was, "Trying to solve traffic congestion by building bigger highways is like trying to solve obesity by buying a bigger belt." He instinctively understood the problems associated with skipping Open. With regard to my daily commute, I skipped Open and went to Resourceful, continuing to look for creative ways to keep doing the same thing (use cheap gas to drive myself to work in a gas-guzzling vehicle) but get different results, even while external conditions were changing around me. I didn't pay attention to the fact that I was slowly putting on weight that could easily be solved by walking to work.

Here's a summary of the predictable consequences of skipping a skill on the compassion cycle.

Skipping this skill	causes these consequences
Openness	• Losing touch with the real needs, concerns, and feelings of others • Loss of morale and engagement • Silos within companies • Incomplete and uninformed solutions that don't work or don't last
Resourcefulness	• Failure to innovate • Loss of initiative • Tradition trumps innovation • Stagnation • Irrelevance
Persistence	• Lack of execution • Poor follow through • Loss of integrity and respect • Low dependability

Following the three rules of the Compassion Cycle is a discipline that requires time and commitment (not to mention a healthy dose of self-compassion as you find yourself staying or skipping a skill on the cycle. It's all part of the process.) Developing the three compassion skills and the discipline to follow these rules opens up tremendous opportunity for engaging in conflict that creates rather than destroys.

Even with these three rules in hand, several critical questions remain:

How do I know if I'm slipping?

How do I know when to move?

How do I make the move from one skill to the next?

In the next chapter, I'll show you how to recognize subtle signs in yourself and others that drama is approaching and what to do about it. Then I'll share our discovery of the Three Choices to Move that enable movement from one compassion skill to the next. Read on to continue your journey of compassionate accountability!

Want to enhance your learning experience?
- Consult the Personal Development Guide in Appendix A, along with your Drama Resilience Assessment profile.

SEVEN

Warning! Drama Approaching!

THREE LEADING INDICATORS

"Everybody has a plan until they get hit."

—Mike Tyson

I get up most days with good intentions. I get up on the right side of the bed, have a positive attitude, and want to do good. I believe most people want to add value in the world. They want to feel confident about who they are. They want to help people become better. They want to be a person others can trust and count on.

And then life happens. Drama comes knocking. Others aren't affirming, don't even try to solve their own problems, and don't follow through on their commitments. The invitations are everywhere: "Hey join the drama party!"

How do you know when you are on the verge of slipping into drama? How do you know it's happening with others? Our team has identified three patterns of behavior that we call Leading Indicators. Subtle changes in behavior, thoughts, feelings, and beliefs signal that a person may be moving from a healthy place within the Compassion Cycle into drama. This usually happens because a person violates one or more of the Three Rules of the Compassion Cycle. These warning signs signal that a compassion skill is slipping and a drama role is lurking in the shadows. The good news is that if we recognize these warning signs early, it's easier to turn things around before there's too much damage.

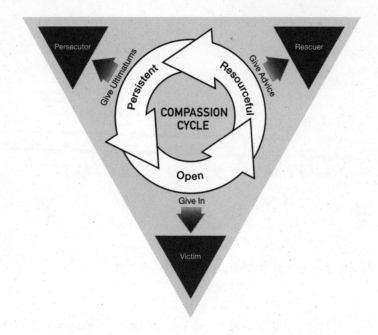

GIVING IN: OPENNESS IS LOSING CONFIDENCE

Open people are skilled at creating harmony and supporting others. For them, giving in is not about healthy compromise. It is about making the decision to concede one's own important boundaries, needs, and wants in order to avoid conflict and "keep the peace." Giving in is usually motivated by fear that conflict would lead to disapproval or rejection by others. The false belief is "I'm only OK if I don't cause any conflict."

Examples:

"Could we turn up the heat if it's OK with everyone else?"

"OK, I'll stay late." (even though **he's missing his daughter's soccer game**)

"I'll just wait here and hope that someone notices that I am alone."

"It's OK, I'm sure you didn't mean to yell at me."

In these examples, the person concedes their comfort, commitments to a child, and boundaries around personal respect in order to avoid potential conflict. Some of these examples may seem more significant and obvious than others. However small it seems, the choice to give in reveals and reinforces a pattern of thoughts, feelings, and behaviors that erodes a person's sense of self-worth. This is fertile soil for Victim myths to take over, "You can make me feel bad emotionally," and "You can make me feel good emotionally" eventually leading to the belief, "I'm not OK. You are OK."

Getting back on the Compassion Cycle requires a return to Openness. This is easier said than done. Because giving in is motivated by a fear of rejection by another person, the solution is to reinforce unconditional worth and self-acceptance. Here are three affirmations you can say to yourself when you start giving in.

"I am OK. My boundaries and needs, feelings and wants matter."

"I am worthy of pursuing what I want, just like anybody else."

"How someone responds to me, even if I don't like it, doesn't define me."

GIVING UNSOLICITED ADVICE: RESOURCEFULNESS IS GETTING COCKY

Resourceful people are skilled at identifying problems and coming up with solutions. Sometimes they get overzealous, usually with good intentions, and offer suggestions without permission from the other party. Giving unsolicited advice stems from the belief, "I know better and you need my help, even if you didn't ask for it." The drive to protect others from their own insufficiencies masks a hidden desire to be perceived as competent and responsible. The belief is, "You will be OK if you take my advice."

Examples:

*"Here, **let me show you** how it's done."*

*"**Why don't you just** tell him to stop?"*

*"**I noticed** that you are rushing every morning to make coffee. **You should** make it the night before."*

*"**See what happens** when you rush?"*

*"Don't you think **it would be better** if you shut your phone down every night?"*

You can probably discern that there are positive motives behind these phrases. Also present is an emerging need to feel justified about being smarter and more capable than the other person. Remember that Resourcefulness emphasizes, "You and I are capable," while unsolicited advice emphasizes, "I am capable and you need my help even if you don't ask for it." The last phrase above illustrates what attorneys call "Leading the witness." Starting a sentence with a negative is a pretty strong sign that you are trying to lead the other person to reach your conclusion. It's how lawyers manipulate others into saying what they want them to say. And non-lawyers do it too!

I want to emphasize that there's nothing wrong with advice, as long as the other person is open to it and has given you permission to offer it. One of the most simple ways to avoid giving unsolicited advice is simply to ask a person if you may share something with them. It's crucial, however, that you do so in a spirit of curiosity, without implying a right or wrong answer, and with full willingness to walk away if they decline your invitation.

If you find yourself giving unsolicited advice, here are three affirmations that can help you turn the ship around and get back on the Compassion Cycle.

I am smart and capable. Others can be as well if I let them.

I am most helpful when people ask me first and are open to my help.

Being available, even without giving advice, is a terrific way to help.

GIVING ULTIMATUMS: PERSISTENCE IS LOSING CONTROL

After hearing Juanita's positive conflict statement at the coffee shop, Sally thought to herself, "If you cared about me, you would realize that Fred is the bad guy here. If you stick up for him, you aren't a good friend." She felt angry and justified just thinking about it. Sally displayed the leading indicator called Giving Ultimatums.

Persistent people pride themselves on finishing what they start and following through on commitments. When frustrated with others who don't seem to be as responsible or trustworthy, they slip towards drama by making unreasonable demands and generalizations. They oversimplify people and their motives, attribute negative intentions, and draw arbitrary lines in the sand to separate who's OK from who isn't OK. Ultimatums are not the same as boundaries. Boundaries are about behavior. Ultimatums are about personal worth. In the previous example, Sally created a situation in her head with faulty logic that allowed her to conclude that Juanita was the problem and therefore Sally didn't need to be responsible for her behavior. Ultimatums are mental gymnastics that allow us to threaten or write somebody off and transform the struggle into an adversarial situation.

Here are some typical Ultimatum phrases:

"Do it or else!"

"That's the last time I trust you."

"If you're late again, you're off the team."

"If you don't finish on time, you're done."

"You WILL be home by seven o'clock."

"I've about had it with this computer."

"You've given me no choice but to fire you."

An ultimatum reflects an attitude that the person is no longer willing or interested in struggling with. They've chosen being justified over being effective. People usually resort to ultimatums because they feel angry, afraid, frustrated, desperate, hurt, or embarrassed and don't have the skill or confidence to do anything else. Fearing that they are losing control, they use ultimatums to cover up the authentic need to be respected and valued.

People who give ultimatums are creating a set-up for failure and trouble because they expect others to take 100-percent of the responsibility for the outcome. The belief is "I am OK. You are not OK." Ironically "struggling with" in compassion involves shared control over outcomes, while giving ultimatums is an expectation that others take on all of the responsibility for the desired outcome. By giving an ultimatum to someone, I've given them complete control over my behavior.

Do you recognize this phrase? "Go ahead, make my day!" Here's the setup.

Clint Eastwood as Harry Callahan in the 1983 movie, *Sudden Impact*, goes into a diner for a morning cup of coffee where he discovers a robbery in progress. He kills all but one of the robbers in a shootout. However, the surviving robber grabs the fleeing waitress, Loretta, holds his gun to her head and threatens to shoot. Instead of backing off, Harry points his .44 Magnum revolver into the boy's face and dares him to shoot, saying between clenched teeth and in his characteristic grumble, "Go ahead, make my day." He means that if the robber attempts to harm Loretta, Harry will be happy to dispatch the robber.[1]

Ultimatums send the message, "If you do XYZ, then I will have every justification to Persecute you."

In college I was the top-seeded player on our tennis team. I wasn't a very compliant, hard working, loyal, or respectful teammate though, and it really bothered my coach. Persistence was important to him and I didn't care much for it. In my junior year, I did something that must have been the last straw for him. He got right up in my face, although he was about four inches shorter than me, and scolded me for my "un-team-like behavior." Red in the face and out of breath, he finished with the ultimatum, "You're done as my number one player until you can learn to show some respect!"

Drama invites drama. I fell for it. Calmly, I responded: "It's obvious, coach, that you haven't learned how to motivate your best player. That's tragic and doesn't reflect well on you." Score! I'd stood up to him, Persecutor to Persecutor.

Dr. Stephen Karpman is famous for saying that in every conflict there's at least 10-percent truth in every position. Coach was at least 10-percent accurate about my behavior. And I'd like to think I was at least 11-percent accurate about my assessment of his coaching ability. I guess I still haven't let it go completely! I won that battle and lost the war. I was demoted on the team and spent the next few weeks earning back trust from my coach and my teammates. I learned a valuable lesson about what happens when two Persecutors compete. Everybody loses no matter how right they are.[2]

If you find yourself giving ultimatums, here are three personal affirmations to help get you back on track.

I'm not a quitter. That's admirable.

By affirming the best in others, I will get their best effort.

Sometimes being effective is better than being right.

Leading Indicators for Drama are like the rumble strips on the side of the road. If you recognize them early and make necessary corrections, damage can be avoided or minimized. Ignoring the warning leads straight to drama and the dance is on! How do the leading indicators show up in your life? What thoughts, feelings, or beliefs let you know you are slipping. What do you want to do to respond positively?

RESPONDING TO LEADING INDICATORS IN OTHERS

In Chapters 9–11 I will provide specific strategies and formulas for responding to full-blown drama. Leading Indicators are drama invitations, not full-blown drama, but certainly on the path. One of the most powerful ways to resist and respond to a leading indicator is with the associated compassion skill. By doing so, you provide an invitation for the person to come back onto the Compassion Cycle. Here are some examples of leading indicators followed by a compassion response.

Leading Indicator Statement	Compassion Invitation
Give In	**Open**
"Could we turn up the heat if it's OK with everyone else?"	"I care about your comfort."
"I don't get it, I'll just wait."	"I hate it when I feel confused."

Leading Indicator Statement	Compassion Invitation
Give Unsolicited Advice "Why don't you just tell him to stop?" "Here, let me show you."	**Resourceful** "If you have experience in similar situations, I'd love to hear what you've tried." "Thanks for your offer. If I have questions, may I ask you for help at that time?"
Give Ultimatums "If you're late again, you're off the team." "You are on thin ice!"	**Persistent** "I'm committed to being on time." "You promised to let me know exactly where I stand."

This strategy won't solve all your problems and it won't magically get people back on track every time. However, it is a robust strategy to resist the temptation of a leading indicator, and invite the other person back into healthy dialogue. What if they continue into the ditch of drama anyway? We have more tools and stronger interventions in the following chapters.

Want to enhance your learning experience?
- Consult the Personal Development Guide in Appendix A, along with your Drama Resilience Assessment profile.

EIGHT

It's All About Choices

THREE CHOICES TO MOVE

"If you don't know where you are going, you are bound to end up where you are headed."

—Chinese Proverb

"If you don't know where you are going, you might wind up someplace else."

—Yogi Berra

"If we don't change direction soon, we'll end up where we're going."

—Professor Irwin Corey

This chapter is about how each individual negotiates the Compassion Cycle. Therefore, throughout the chapter, you have my permission to focus on you. Entirely. Don't worry about anyone else.

Since this chapter is about personal choices and consequences, I'd also like to make a request. Would you please avoid applying this chapter to anyone else but yourself?

We are all headed on the trajectory of inertia. Without adding the energy of intention and choice to combat this inertia, we will end up where we've always been, in the same corners, same drama alliances, and same struggles we've played out thousands of times before. When we don't take responsibility for our choices, habit wins.

Humans are agentic beings. This means we are agents. We have the capacity to envision what we want, set our sights on those things, and exert energy towards getting them. This is why life is about choices. Staying on the Compassion Cycle, resisting the pull of drama, and moving forward bring us face to face with several critical forks in the road. These choice points require us to figure out what we want and make several important decisions about those goals. The question isn't whether we will make the choice. The question is which choice will we make, which path we will take.

Each point on the Compassion Cycle has a purpose. When that purpose is fulfilled, it's time to move. Lingering after the purpose has been achieved is a recipe for stagnation and drama. To move requires a choice. Making the healthy choice advances us along the Compassion Cycle and prepares us for the next step. Avoiding the choice increases our chance of falling into a drama role. Let's take a look at the purpose of each compassion skill, the choice to move, and what happens if we don't make the choice.

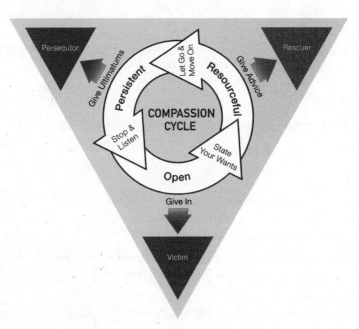

OPENNESS AND THE POWER OF ASKING

The purpose of Openness is to experience, understand, and affirm your emotional world. It's about creating a safe place to discover what's important to you and what you want. Once you have identified your emotional experience and your intentions regarding it, the purpose has been fulfilled. I'm not refer-ring to some profound realization or uncovering of some deep secret. It is as simple as getting to the point where you can identify a feeling you are having, understand the importance of this feeling for you, and get some sense of where you'd like to go with it. Some examples:

> *"I'm feeling **anxious** (emotion) about this transition and **would really like some clarity** (intention)."*

> *"I'm **angry** (emotion) with you and **want to work through it** (intention)."*

> *"I'm feeling **frustrated** (emotion) about my phone and **want to be able to rely on it** (intention)."*

> *"I **care** a lot (emotion) about you and **want to help** (intention)."*

Generally, you know you are ready to move beyond Openness when you can articulate an important feeling you have and your intention for how you'd like to feel or do something differently in the future. Openness is not about problem-solving or dictating specifics, it's about stating a desired feeling or goal. In the above examples, the desired goals aren't specific to tasks or parameters. Instead, they are a verbalization of intentions. It's about "What do I want?" not "How will I get it?" Remember, Openness is Open!

STATE YOUR WANTS: MAKE THE CHOICE TO OWN YOUR POTENCY
Once you've identified and stated your intention, you are ready to ask for what you want. Asking for help or support in pursuing your intention is an affirmation of your worthiness. We call it "owning your potency." This is what distinguishes wishing from pursuing. I can wish for a reliable phone or the opportunity to help my colleague through a tough time. That doesn't make it happen. Sharing what I want or need to get closer to that goal is the critical next step to turn my intention into something more. Let's take the previous statements one step further by stating my wants.

*"I'm feeling **anxious** (emotion) about this transition and **would really like some clarity** (intention). Will you **help me work through this** (ask)?"*

*"I'm **angry** (emotion) with you and **want to work through it** (intention). Are you willing to **talk about it with me** (ask)?"*

*"I'm **frustrated** (emotion) about my phone and **want to be able to rely on it** (intention). Will you **help me problem-solve this** (ask)?"*

*"I **care** a lot (emotion) about you and **want to help** (intention). How can **I support you** (ask)?"*

Why state your wants? Why ask for help? Why engage another person? Here are a few reasons. You might be able to think of others. Stating your wants;

- Affirms that you are worthy of another person's time, energy, and attention.
- Reinforces that your needs, feelings, and goals matter.
- Builds healthy relationships when done with compassion.
- Gives others more awareness of how they can be helpful.
- Can preempt Rescuing behavior from others.
- Helps preempt your own Rescuing behavior.

AVOIDING THE CHOICE TO STATE YOUR WANTS: HEADING TOWARD VICTIM

What if you don't ask for what you want? What we've discovered is that people who don't ask for what they want usually end up in the Victim role. There are many excuses and justifications, a lot of negative self-talk and fears that crop up.

"What if they reject me?"

"It won't make a difference."

"I never get what I want anyway."

"They won't care."

Probe people about their excuses and they will defend them. They can cite historical data to back it up. They believe they are making the calculated, correct choice.[1] Most of their arguments are contaminated with myths, just like each of the statements above. Many people fear that asking for what they want makes them too vulnerable and is a set-up for disappointment. This is true only if you believe the myth, "others can make me feel good or bad emotionally." What are your excuses for not stating your wants? What myths are holding you back?

Openness is about recognizing that I am worthy. Therefore, sharing what I want is simply the next step to demonstrate to myself and others that this is true. How the other person responds does not dictate the value of my feelings or intentions. It may influence my next choice, but it doesn't define me.

Stating what you want is the bridge that takes you to Resourcefulness. At Resourcefulness you can begin working toward a solution. Avoiding the choice is the slippery slope back to the role of Victim.

RESOURCEFULNESS AND THE POWER OF LETTING GO

The purpose of Resourcefulness is to understand the situation or problem and figure out options and action steps for moving forward. Via collaborative problem-solving around what's most important, you get one step closer to what you want. Resourcefulness gets you to a point where any or all of the following conditions are met:

- You understand the situation or problem.
- You have generated several good options.
- More information won't make the decision any easier.
- You have weighed the pros and cons of various options.
- You have a strategy that's ready to implement.
- Trying something will teach you much more than further thinking about it.

At this point, all that's left is a decision. Which option will I choose? What action will I take? Will I begin implementing the plan? You know you've been successful at Resourceful if you can say things like;

"I understand my options and the pros and cons of each one."

"There are three things I could do to advance my objectives."

"The plan is ready to execute."

LET GO AND MOVE ON: MAKE THE CHOICE TO GRIEVE LOSS

This is where things get tough for a lot of people. Generating options is fun. Brainstorming ideas is energizing. Researching is rewarding. Developing amazing strategic plans looks great on paper. Exploring pros and cons can be stimulating. And all of this only gets you up to the starting line for Persistence. Resourcefulness is like preparation for a race. It's not the race.

Consultants provide expert recommendations. Analysts show patterns and predict potential outcomes. Learning generates new ideas. And still, none of this is implementation. Making the choice to act is a powerful, scary, and exhilarating decision. Some people make it easily. Some become completely overwhelmed by the choice. There is loss associated with making a choice, and this is difficult for some.

I love buffets, any kind. I've never met a buffet I didn't exploit. I used to think it was because I loved food so much. I grew up in several countries and have developed an expansive palette. So I reasoned that I liked buffets because I just like to try lots of different foods. Recently I've discovered that my attraction to buffets may go a little deeper. The truth is, I don't like to choose among options. I have a very difficult time ordering off a menu. I can't decide what I want. I check with others to see if we could "share a couple things" so I can try more than one menu item. I look for the combo plate. If the restaurant doesn't have one, I often attempt to customize the options to get greater choices. Sometimes I just order several appetizers. My last resort tactic is to ask the server to surprise me and choose something for me. This way I can avoid responsibility for my choice.

This habit wreaks havoc on my waistline. And I think it all stems from my difficulty letting go and moving on. I worry that the other person's food might end up tasting better than mine and then I would be disappointed. I worry that the option I don't choose might have been the better one. It's crazy-making!

Avoiding the choice to take action, let go, and move on costs companies billions of dollars a year in the form of lost opportunities, resources wasted in predictive analyses, and bringing in more consultants whose recommendations are never implemented. How is it that people, teams, and organizations can put so much into planning, learning, and organizing yet avoid taking the leap to implementation? We've discovered several reasons, and they all lead back to loss.

Loss of control: Once I take action, I've lost some control over what might happen. If I keep thinking, I don't have to experience the unknown that accompanies doing. If I keep talking, I can avoid finding out how someone will react to what I've shared. If I keep analyzing, I can avoid the loss of control over what happens next. Loss of control is scary and pushes many people and organizations to turn around, re-group, or simply skip Persistence altogether. Do you fear the loss of control that often comes with making a decision?

Loss of options: Once I choose the turkey breast, I've lost the option of nachos. Once we transition to InfusionSoft as our Customer Relationship Management tool, we've lost the option of using MailChimp. Once I agree to the price of this car, I've lost the option to negotiate a lower price. The loss of "what could have been" keeps many people up at night. Regrets and second-guessing is an energy vampire that keeps us from letting go and moving on.

One year during the Christmas holiday, my oldest daughter needed to make a decision about a summer youth mission trip. The reservations needed to be made and deposits submitted six months in advance. The mission trip conflicted with church camp. The pros and cons were clear. She had everything she needed to make the decision. And she couldn't. I found her curled up in a ball in her bed, sobbing. I asked her what was wrong. She explained, "If I do the mission trip then I will miss church camp. If I go to camp I'll miss the mission trip. I can't decide."

Do you struggle with the loss of options that will disappear if you make a choice?

Loss of certainty: Moving from planning to doing makes it real. It opens up a host of unknown variables. Anything could happen. This uncertainty is frightening. I remember the first time I jumped off the high-diving board at the neighborhood pool. I stood there for what seemed like hours, staring down at the water a million miles away. My friends yelled, taunted, and reassured me. The kids behind me got impatient. I climbed back down the ladder several times, too scared to take the plunge. I re-assessed the situation, asked others about their experience, practiced "slapping my feet" against the water to simulate the impact I might experience. None of it helped. There came a point where nothing else I did could take the fear away. Nothing else could close the gap that remained between what I knew and where I needed to go. I didn't jump that day.

Here's the crux; loss is an emotional issue. It cannot be solved with logic. The best that Resourcefulness can do is drop you off at the bridge of loss. Only grief will take you across the bridge to Persistence.

People avoid the choice to let go and move on because they don't want to feel the discomfort of loss. Until we authentically experience and appreciate the loss associated with making the choice to let go and move on, we can't fully transition from Resourcefulness to Persistence. When you want to support others who are facing this kind of loss, avoid making the following types of statements; they don't help because none of them validate the loss associated with making a choice to let go and move on.

"Just do it."

"In a week it will seem like nothing."

"We simply have to make a decision!"

"What's the big deal?"

"There's always next time."

When you're facing the need to let go and move on, you need to recognize the decision you make and the consequences that go with it, as well as the loss of options not chosen and doors that have been closed. Here are some examples that demonstrate a person is letting go and moving on:

"Yes, I will marry you. And by doing this I accept the responsibility of a lifelong commitment to you. I also grieve some loss of freedom that I had before."

"I will choose to switch IT providers because I know we need more capacity. I realize that the learning curve will be steep and this will be very hard work. I am sad to lose the relationship and dependability we had with our old provider."

"I am going to let Gary go. I accept the consequences of waiting so long to make the decision. I feel badly about the time and opportunity we lost by delaying an inevitable outcome."

Resourcefulness is about recognizing that I am capable. Choosing to let go and move on is simply the next step to demonstrate to myself and others that this is true. Capability is fully manifested when I take responsibility for my choices and they are converted into action.

AVOIDING THE CHOICE TO LET GO AND MOVE ON: HEADING TOWARD RESCUER

Many times people appear to be making change, but it doesn't stick. Organizations seem to be taking three steps forward, only to find themselves four steps back. Often this is because the transition from Resourceful to Persistent is forced or skipped without taking the time and energy to grieve the loss and let go. When people hold onto the emotional baggage of unresolved grief, it reduces their ability to engage fully in Persistent action.

Avoiding the choice to let go and move on usually results in a reinvestment in Resourcefulness, which can easily slip into Rescuing. Instead of dealing with my own insecurity over moving forward, I reinforce the value of staying right where I am. I become the intellectual expert, giving everybody advice on how to do it. These are Rescuer tactics to justify my own inability to stay on the Compassion Cycle. Rescuing undermines your capability and avoids responsibility for owning your choices.

Do you have difficulty making decisions among options? Do you struggle to take action even when you know it's the right thing to do? Maybe unrecognized grief and loss is getting in the way. It's OK to say goodbye to what could have been. It's OK to feel sad about the road not taken. Instead of wondering what could have been, it's OK to bid that option farewell and grieve the loss. Most importantly, take responsibility for the choice you make, the consequences of that choice, and the sadness it involves.

CASE STUDY: DAN, THE CEO WHO COULDN'T LET GO AND MOVE ON

Dan Stutterheim is president and CEO of KASA Companies, a manufacturer of automation and industrial control systems. As long as he can remember, he thought that leading by example was sufficient to get people to do things. This makes sense because he's in his late 40s, a crossover between Baby Boomers and the Generation X. He grew up in a Midwestern, conservative culture with a strong work ethic in which you lived your values, and actions spoke louder than words. His father owned the company before him and believed that leading by example was enough.

Dan also spent many years responding to conflict by adopting the Persecutor or Rescuer role. This is the most typical leader mentality in the manufacturing culture. It's a rough-and-tumble world with no minced words and no soft edges. Over time, Dan got tired. He became worn out from the self-imposed pressure to supply all the answers and the stress of negative conflict. Something changed inside him: he realized that he didn't want to be a leader who had all the answers and was feared. Instead, he wanted to be the kind of person who was a respected mentor and advisor. He wanted to develop his people and help them take ownership of their own stuff—both the positive and the negative.

From then on, Dan worked toward abstinence from drama behaviors and attitudes. For the most part, he was successful. He was kinder, gentler, and probably less stressed, and, over time, he found that he had lost something when he gave up drama. Much like an addict loses predictability and satisfaction when he gives up his vice, Dan felt something was missing. A recent interaction with one of his team members illustrates the problem.

KASA Companies had implemented a new system of compensation and a new bonus structure for its high-level employees, and was seeking to get those employees to sign a legal document relating to this change. The employees were not required to sign the document, but if they did not, they were not guaranteed certain privileges and rights within the new compensation system. One of Dan's team members, a person with whom he had long struggled to connect, didn't want to sign it. We'll call him Gordon. The two became engaged in a debate of logic and "reasons for or against." Dan hated the stress of this conflict, and truly believed that signing the document would be the best course of action for Gordon. Dan stewed and fretted about this situation and tried everything he could think of to convince Gordon to sign the document. One evening he stayed late preparing logic and arguments about the benefits of the new system. He poured over past productivity numbers, ran some projections, and reviewed the policy one more time. He even prepared talking points for when he met with Gordon. It made no difference. Gordon still refused to sign. All of Dan's efforts had only increased the distance between him and Gordon. For a company owner whose mission was to make KASA a great place to work, Dan was failing with his own people.

After completing our Leading Out of Drama® training, Dan had an epiphany. "I'm stuck at Resourceful," he told me. "I keep trying to problem-solve Gordon's resistance and figure out how to persuade him to voluntarily accept this new system." I asked Dan why he was stuck, what was keeping him from going to Persistence. He explained, "Persistence feels like being a dictator. I wish people would just follow me because of my brilliance, ideas, motivation, and experience. But it's not sufficient. It's not Gordon that needs to let go and move on. It's me." Dan wanted to be a hero who could magnificently gain buy-in, could offer brilliant insights, and was deemed a great leader by others. Dan was facing two important deficits in his leadership skill set; the skill to let go and move on, and the skill of healthy Persistence.

First, Dan realized that trying to persuade Gordon to change his mind was fruitless. He had no control over Gordon's attitude and needed to accept this and move on. This required a process of grieving the loss of his false expectation that logic and role-modeling could make another person do something. If it wasn't mandatory that employees sign the agreement, why was he so invested in Gordon signing it? Dan realized that it was because of his pride around being an expert and because he equated rejection of the agreement as a rejection of him. If one of his own team members didn't sign, what did that say about his credibility as a leader? Again, Dan knew he needed to let go and move on, grieve the loss of control over how other people think or act, and focus on himself. He needed to stop giving others the power to determine his OK-ness.

The second decision was to embrace healthy Persistence. For Dan this meant getting clear about what he wanted, what was at stake, and what battles were not worth fighting. So Dan brought Gordon into his office one more time. But in this meeting, Dan made no use of logic, dispensed with talking points, and had no expectations. He simply stated, "I respect your decision, Gordon. I've been trying too hard to get you to do something you don't want to do. I'm sorry. I do want you to know that the old system is gone. The new system is here to stay. I can't make you sign the document and it's not mandatory as part of your employment here. And, I want you to be clear about the consequences if you don't sign it. Do you have any questions?"

Gordon didn't have any questions. He thanked Dan and still didn't sign the agreement. He accepted the consequences and moved on. The two men engaged in no further conflict around this issue. Dan felt as if a great weight had been lifted.

Are you a leader who's gotten stuck, unable to let go, and focusing on the wrong things? Do you worry about whether your time and energy are making any difference? Do you have a history of conflict with casualties that you'd prefer not to repeat? Is the inability to let go keeping you from learning new skills for positive conflict?

If you answered "yes" to any of these questions, you aren't alone. Dan is just like many top leaders with a big heart who are trying to build healthy companies. The problem Dan faced, and the reason I wrote this book, is that healthy companies require conflict to thrive—conflict without casualties.

When I coach leaders who recognize they are in the same place Dan was, I explain my role with a simple analogy. I invite them to think of me as the tires or hay bales stacked up at the most dangerous corner on the racetrack. Sometimes my most important job is to keep them from crashing as they practice coming around the bend of Resourcefulness or Persistence without sliding off into Drama. The curves never become less dangerous, but the driver gets better and better at navigating the course.

PERSISTENCE AND THE POWER OF STOPPING TO LISTEN

The purpose of Persistence is to follow through, period. Ideally, promises should be kept, decisions should be implemented, targets should be pursued, and difficulties should be endured. It's very difficult to know who we are or what we are made of until we're tested. Until we are faced with obstacles, we don't know how important our goals are. Unless we persevere, we don't know how much we value something.

Being successful at Persistence requires a single-minded focus. It requires tuning out distractions, staying focused on the goal, and conserving energy for what's most important. Anyone who has pursued excellence in their field understands how important focus is for success. Distractions and diversions are a threat to follow-through.

Persistence also requires the discipline of consistency and repetition, which can be kind of boring. Persistence isn't as fun or exciting as Resourcefulness. It's not as warm and fuzzy as Openness. Yet success depends very much on doing the hard things really well, every time. This repetition and discipline builds habits that make it easier and more automatic.

STOP AND LISTEN: MAKE THE CHOICE TO PRACTICE EMPATHY

The only way to keep Persistence from mutating into Persecuting is to return to Openness. This requires stopping so you can hear what's going on around you and inside of you. Lift your nose from the grindstone, turn off the computer, put the smartphone away, and stop doing. Try this little exercise. Follow the instructions below, in the order listed.

- Find a quiet place where you won't be distracted for at least 10 minutes.
- Remove distractions such as your phone.
- Sit comfortably.
- Close your eyes.
- Take five deep breaths.
- Listen to your heart. Can you feel it? How fast is it beating? What emotions are you experiencing? Are you relaxed? Anxious? Agitated? Enthusiastic?
- Listen to your body. How do you feel? Any tension? Aches or pains? Heartburn? How did you sleep last night?
- Listen to your soul. Do you have a purpose? Are you fulfilled? Are you tending to the most important things?
- Reflect on these questions: What is your heart, body, and soul telling you? Have you tuned these messages out? What price are you paying for staying at Persistence?

The pharmaceutical industry is making a killing off of people who stay at Persistence too long. Heartburn, sleep problems, sexual dysfunction, anxiety, headaches, chronic pain, digestive problems and depression can all result from the stress of persisting too hard and long. There's probably a pill or supplement that can make your symptoms go away, or at least keep them quiet for now.

Or, you could stop, listen, and practice empathy by taking caring of yourself.

It's hard to stop. It's hard to press "pause" on a project in order to refuel, recharge and reconnect. Yet, this is often the only way to get perspective and keep myths from creeping in. Here are some statements that reveal a person is making the choice to stop and listen:

"I have been working too hard and I'm tired. I'm not sleeping well."

"We've been pushing really hard on this project for the last quarter. Let's use our next project meeting to just step back and see how everybody is doing. No project talk."

"I have been really short with my wife lately. I've let the upcoming merger consume me, even when I'm at home."

"I've gained a bunch of weight in the last year and I'm taking blood pressure medication. My doctor says it's because of stress. She's right. I need to slow down."

Stopping and listening could reveal a ton of things that could help you. It can help you recalibrate. Building in time to practice exercises like the previous one can help you get back to Openness on a regular basis and keep the cycle moving. The benefits of stopping and listening are powerful. For example, you can:

- Detect early warning signs of physical, emotional, social, or spiritual problems
- Evaluate the overall success of your efforts
- Recalibrate your expectations
- Maintain strong connections with important people in your life
- Adjust priorities if needed
- Adjust strategies if needed
- Gain perspective on what's most important

AVOIDING THE CHOICE TO STOP AND LISTEN: HEADING TO PERSECUTOR

Persistence is a powerful and important component of success. Many would say it's the most important. It depends how you look at it. Persistence is absolutely necessary to see things through, give plans a chance to succeed, earn trust, and move your goals forward. And, there's a downside. I've extracted a few words and phrases from the previous few paragraphs.

Single-minded
Tune out
Distractions are a threat
Repetition
Habits
Automatic

The biggest problem with Persistence is that it's not Open. In many ways, Openness is one of the biggest threats to Persistence. Persistence tunes out distractions, while Openness embraces novelty. Persistence keeps working toward a goal, while Openness revels in the moment. Persistence focuses on task completion, while Openness focuses on affirming people. Persistence says "don't stop until you are done," while Openness says, "stop and smell the roses."

A family was driving from Wyoming to Arizona on vacation. A tire blew on their car and they had to pull over on the highway. Unfortunately, they had left the spare in their garage to make room for their extra luggage. What to do? Noticing a sign for a service station a half-mile ahead, the parents and their two teenage children decided to push the car rather than spend extra money and time calling a tow truck. Working together as a family, they developed a way to keep the car slowly moving along the median strip. Several hours later they arrived at the exit for the gas station, tired but feeling a sense of accomplishment. Even more powerful, though, was the stress Dad was experiencing from the delay. He decided that he didn't have time to stop at the service station. "We are going slow, but at least we're moving forward," he announced. "We don't have time to stop, or we won't make it to our destination."

The danger of Persistence is that we get so focused on our goals, mission priorities, strategic plans, and action steps that we lose focus on the world around us and within us. We lose touch with hugely valuable information that could affect our success. Remember that Persistence addresses the issue of whether we are accountable. Accountability has two components. I can be accountable for my behavior, which is the typical task-oriented component. And I can also be accountable to others, which is the relationship-oriented component. Stopping to listen recognizes the vital relationship-oriented duty of Persistence.

I've heard of artists so engrossed in their work that they go several days without eating or sleeping. I've heard of people driving cars so long and fast that they overheat. I've heard of people who focus so much on getting the next promotion that they lose their family. I've heard of people who put so much pressure on themselves to keep promises that they have a stroke. Persistence is hard on the body and soul. Over time, it takes a toll.

As I described in Chapter 5 regarding the rise and fall of civilizations, our human propensity to get stuck at Persistence and head to Persecutor seems to cause many of our problems. The power of moving back to Open is one big reason why the Cycle of Compassion can transform both how we do relation-ships and how we do business.

A NESTED CONSTELLATION

The Cycle of Compassion can move very quickly. Juanita made a whole trip around it in one single statement to Sally at the coffee shop. A basketball player may make one trip around it each day during practice. I cycle through it with each agenda item during a staff meeting, even as the overall structure of the meeting follows an O-R-P-O template. A company launching a new change initiative may cycle through once a month. The pace is determined by the situation, when it's time to move, and how well each person makes the transition.

I'm reminded of the classic art game called Spirograph. I grew up with Spirograph in the 1970s. I loved the amazing designs I could create by poking different colored pens through holes around the edge of notched gears and follow circular patterns. Many of my creations involved cycles within cycles, in different sizes but identical patterns, elegantly nested within an overall constellation.

The Compassion Cycle allows individuals and groups to negotiate multiple conflict and change situations at micro and macro levels, internally and with others, much like a Spirograph. In this book we are building a framework and toolkit for transforming negative drama into compassionate accountability. Developing your compassion skills, adhering to the rules of the Compassion Cycle, and making the key choices to move are all pieces of the puzzle. Any one of them will make a positive impact. Using them together is powerful and transformative.

Want to enhance your learning experience?
- Consult the Personal Development Guide in Appendix A, along with your Drama Resilience Assessment profile.

NINE

Coaching Accountability When There's No Drama

MATCH AND MOVE

Sally's friend Juanita doesn't spend much time in drama. She avoids drama allies and adversaries, she keeps herself from joining others in drama, she follows the three rules of Compassionate Conflict, and she regularly makes Choices to Move. Juanita is a beacon of compassion.

Juanita is the VP of Marketing at Compassion Corp, a competitor of Drama Corp that has been rapidly gaining traction in their market. Juanita is responsible for a team of 26 people who have learned that she doesn't play the game of drama. Neither does she tolerate it from her team.

Is life perfect in the marketing department at Compassion Corp? Of course not. Nobody is perfect. However, the rules of engagement are consistent with the Compassion Cycle. Juanita makes sure her team has the role-modeling, training, and support they need to follow these rules in their behavior with each other and their clients.

On any given day there's not a lot of drama, but there's plenty of positive conflict. Juanita believes that positive conflict is a necessary part of creativity, innovation, and engagement. In fact, Juanita initiates conflict on a regular basis with her people, all for one driving reason: to coach her employees towards personal accountability while advancing team goals.

When there's no drama, Juanita uses a strategy called "Match and Move" to keep her team progressing around the Compassion Cycle. The purpose of Match and Move is to meet people where they are on the Compassion Cycle and facilitate the appropriate Choice to Move. Great leaders, mentors, coaches, and other facilitative leaders seek opportunities to meet people where they are and struggle with them towards higher levels of performance, accountability, and maturity. Match and Move is a highly effective and easily-learned coaching technique for helping people accomplish these goals.

In the last chapter, I encouraged readers to keep the focus on themselves. In this chapter, the same concepts are applied to interpersonal relationships. Once you've gotten a handle on your own process of making the Choices to Move, it can be used very effectively with others as well.

MEETING PEOPLE WHERE THEY ARE

I was first introduced to this concept in my previous life as a therapist. My mentor and supervisor, Dr. Larry Hays, PhD, was a very wise and experienced clinician with a big heart. He sketched for me two diagrams representing two different philosophies of helping. In the first diagram, the black line represents the helper (therapist, coach, mentor). The gray line represents the client. This traditional intervention philosophy suggests that the helper sets the standard, gives advice to the client, and the client makes positive changes to align with the helper. In this paradigm, the helper is the expert, the role model, and the evaluator of the client's progress.

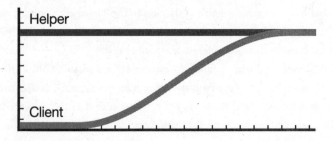

In the second diagram the helper joins the client, seeking to understand his or her frame of reference, validate his or her worldview, and affirm his or her experience. Together, then, the two move forward on a journey. The helper facilitates growth and learning but doesn't direct it. Sometimes, the helper grows more than the client. Together, their trajectory of positive change is much steeper than in the first diagram.

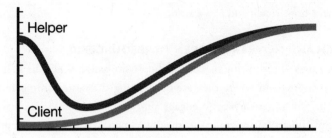

In this more contemporary paradigm, the helper is a coach, facilitator, and co-creator on the journey. Dr. Hays subscribed to the second philosophy. That's what he taught me and the research backs it up. Clinical outcomes research shows the second philosophy of treatment is superior in terms of symptom improvement, increased self-efficacy, and healthy, autonomous functioning.

These diagrams and Dr. Hays' philosophy made a big impression on me and continues to influence the work I do with Next Element. Looking back, I now see that these diagrams represent a drama versus compassion approach to helping. The traditional paradigm is fraught with drama. The professional gives advice, plays the role of the expert Rescuer, puts themselves in a position above the person receiving help, and is not Open. The other paradigm is full of compassion concepts, including starting at Open, struggling with, an attitude of "I'm OK. You're OK," and respecting the autonomy of the person seeking help.

Modern-day coaching is a lot like Dr. Hays' philosophy, which is maybe why it's taken off around the world as an effective alternative to therapy. Coaching is about meeting the client where they are and helping them to succeed at their goals. We've experienced a lot of success applying the Compassion Cycle principles to coaching. Our clients learn to embrace that they are worthwhile, capable, and accountable. We struggle with them. As coaches, consultants, trainers, and facilitators, we rely on the Compassion Cycle to help us avoid slipping into drama.

Regardless of what kind of change agent you are, whether a leader, mentor, coach, parent, or facilitator, Match and Move is a great technique to meet people where they are and struggle with them towards higher levels of performance, accountability, and maturity. Remember that Match and Move is used only when someone is in the Compassion Cycle, exhibiting one of the three compassion skills. For addressing drama with positive conflict, we have discovered a highly effective strategy that we'll share in the next chapter.

Here's how Match and Move works.

MATCH AND MOVE FROM OPEN TO RESOURCEFUL

When a person is showing one of the three compassion skills, the best thing to do is meet them where they are by showing the same compassion skill yourself. This is a great way to engage another person, build rapport, show empathy, and get into alignment with another person before you start positive conflict and ask for increased accountability. I've used similar concepts, such as mirroring or active listening.[1] These are good strategies and do not contradict Compassion Matching. However, through our team's research we've found that the precision and effectiveness of these strategies can be enhanced considerably by matching the process and content of what is said to the compassion skill of the other person. Let's say Juanita's employee, Brian, comes to her office and shares the following:

> *"I am anxious about the upcoming merger. There are so many unknowns."*

The first thing Juanita does is diagnose whether Brian is in drama or not. She assesses that there is no drama: He is simply stating his feelings and why he feels the way he does. Since there's no drama, Juanita identifies the compassion skill Brian is exhibiting. In this case, it is Openness. He is disclosing a difficult emotion to her. Recall that there are three ways to be Open: empathize through personal experience; validate another's emotions, needs, and motives; and disclose feelings, needs, and motives.

Juanita has choices about which of the three types of Openness she wants to use to match Brian. In this case, any of the three might work.

> *"I hear you. This reminds me of when we got our new CEO three years ago. I was worried for a week wondering how things were going to shake out with my job."* (Empathize)

> *"It's perfectly normal to feel anxious. You're not alone."* (Validate)

> *"I'm feeling anxious too, and I want all of us to feel more confident."* (Disclose)

Juanita could share all three of these responses if she wanted, or just one or two. Just because Brian disclosed doesn't mean Juanita has to. In fact, it might be better if she affirmed the feelings that Brian shared. How much compassion matching you engage in depends on the situation. Situations that are more emotionally charged or where the stakes are higher might require more matching than others. The best way to know if your compassion match was effective is whether the person accepts your invitation to make the Choice to Move. That's what comes next.

If you are at high risk for drama-based helping, you may be good at the compassion match, but then you'll be tempted to start offering assistance in ways that aren't helpful. I applaud your intentions, and if you head into drama before you act on your intentions, it won't turn out well. We covered that in the chapter on Drama-Based Helping.

If you want to be helpful and encourage the other person to take responsibility for themselves, the best thing you can do is invite the Choice to Move.

After Openness, the choice is to State Your Wants. Letting people know what you want and asking for help is how you take responsibility for what's been revealed at Open. So the "Move" part in Match and Move is to invite and facilitate the other person to make the choice to reveal what they want. Here's what it might look like for Juanita.

> *"I'm feeling anxious too, and I want all of us to feel more confident."* (Disclose.) *"Is there anything you want from me?"* (Invite Brian to state his wants)

> *"I hear you. This reminds me of when we got our new CEO three years ago. I was worried for a week wondering how things were going to shake out with my job."* (Empathize.) *"If there's anything I can do to help, will you let me know?"* (Invite Brian to state his wants)

> *"It's perfectly normal to feel anxious. You're not alone."* (Validate.) *"Is there anything I can do to help?"* (Invite Brian to state his wants)

Notice that Juanita never foists any specific type of help on Brian. She never suggests what Brian should do, and never takes action without being asked. The key to inviting the Choice to State Your Wants is to keep the responsibility on the other person. If Juanita were to take over responsibility for Brian's feelings, wants or motives, she would have violated his OK-ness and entered into drama-based helping. Here are some examples of what many of us say that's not helpful.

> *"Don't feel anxious Brian. It will be fine in a week."* (Rescuing by re-defining Brian's feelings)

> *"Just try to ignore it. There's nothing you can do about it anyway."* (Rescuing by giving unsolicited advice)

> *"I'll talk to the department head and see what I can find out about your job."* (Victim helping by putting oneself in the line of fire and taking over action on behalf of the other person)

> *"Oh no, I'm so sorry. I will be sure to let you know whatever I find out about job assignments."* (Victim helping by compromising one's boundaries and maybe even breaking rules in order to help)

The bottom line is that until Brian states his wants and takes ownership over his needs and feelings, it's inappropriate and unhelpful for Juanita to provide help. All it does is reinforce dependence and drama-based relationships. Many consultants think they're supporting an individual by Matching, then heading straight to drama-based helping. They empathize with and validate our suffering, then start trying to fix the problem without our permission or involvement.

By following her Open Match with invitations for Brian to make the Choice to State Your Wants, Juanita reinforces several critical ground rules of compassionate accountability cultures and relationships.

1. I care about you and am willing to help you.
2. I won't do it for you.
3. You are worthwhile and responsible for your feelings, needs, and wants.

Now the ball is in Brian's court. Brian might or might not accept the ground rules. If he does, he will respond in a way that lets Juanita know he's made the Choice to Move. It might sound like,

"Thanks Juanita. I will definitely ask you for help."

"I appreciate your offer to help. May I ask you some questions about the merger and how it affects my job?"

"Thanks for the support. I just need someone who will listen. Will you do that?"

Any of these responses advances this conversation to Resourceful, where the new purpose will be to problem-solve what Brian has asked for. If Juanita means what she said, she'll follow through on her invitation unless it violates one of her non-negotiables. We'll get to that later. This shows Brian that he can count on her to be there for him and support his personal responsibility at the same time.

Brian might shy away from the invitation, or ignore it completely. Invitations to make a Choice to Move create conflict because at a process level they invite us to take responsibility for our feelings and behavior. Invitations aren't always easy to accept, especially if a person doesn't want to take personal responsibility. Brian could say something like:

"I don't know what to do, I'm just so anxious."

"Thanks for the offer, but I gotta figure this out on my own."

What should Juanita do in this situation? If Brian stays out of drama, and stays at Open, all she can do is repeat the Match and Move strategy. She can't force Brian to move. She can only invite. Whether or not he accepts the invitation doesn't change his accountability for behavior or performance. Nor does it absolve Juanita of her responsibility to hold him accountable for his performance. If he tries to tough it out and figure it out on his own, that's his choice. However, if failing to ask for help compromises his performance or behavior, he is still responsible. Juanita has another powerful strategy at her disposal that we'll cover in later chapters.

Here are some handy ways to Match and Move at Open even when a person doesn't accept your invitation.

"I care about you and I'm here for you if you want help."

"I'm concerned because I can see you are struggling. If you change your mind, I'm available."

If Brian doesn't accept Juanita's invitation and stays out of drama, Juanita can wrap up the conversation with something like the statements above, then go about her day. She will remain willing and available to help Brian. If Brian comes to her later and asks for help, she won't hold it against him and will avoid drama-based cheap shots like, "I figured you'd come around," or "See, I was right." If Brian goes into drama, Juanita has another strategy. It's called the Formula for Compassionate Conflict. If you want to read ahead, skip to the next chapter.

Here are some Openness Match phrases that may come in handy as you develop and practice your own repertoire:

"Your feelings matter."

"I care about you."

"I can appreciate how difficult this is."

"I remember feeling like this."

"It's OK to feel this way."

And, some additional invitations to make the Choice to State your Wants.

"What do you want most?"

"If you want anything, it's OK to ask."

"Can I help?"

"Do you want any help?"

"How would you like to feel instead?"

"In a perfect world, how would you like to feel?"

MATCH AND MOVE FROM RESOURCEFUL TO PERSISTENT: INVITING THE CHOICE TO LET GO AND MOVE ON

Matching someone at Resourceful follows the same principle we just explored, and has a very different feel from matching at Open. Resourceful is about curious learning and creative problem-solving. You can identify when someone is at Resourceful if they are exchanging information, exploring options, asking curious questions, or generating possibilities. Later in the day, one of Juanita's brightest creative minds, Javier, catches her in the hall and says,

> *"I just checked our analytics for November and our click-through rate on the new website ad is up 33-percent from last month."*

Sounds like good news, right? Juanita could simply acknowledge what she heard with a quick, "Great job, Javier!" or "Thanks for letting me know." Positive affirmation could be extremely motivating for Javier. So there's no reason for Juanita not to do it. In fact, we recommend leaders put a lot more energy into positively motivating their employees. It's a huge driver of performance and morale.[2]

What if Juanita wants more from Javier? What if she also wants to capitalize on this opportunity to clarify action steps and accountabilities? Juanita never misses a chance to reinforce the ground rules of compassionate accountability. So, after offering Javier a positive affirmation, she applies Match and Move.

> *"That's terrific, Javier. If I recall, that's 10-percent more than our target goal. Will you let me know if there's anything we should we change in our strategy because of this?"*

Juanita matched Javier at Resourceful by exchanging relevant information. Then she invited him to let go and move on with the question, "Is there anything we should change in our strategy because of this?" The question invites Javier to move beyond knowing, and translate the knowledge of a 33-percent gain into action. Here's another example:

> *"Great job Javier. We have data on three different ads now. Will you recommend which one we should use for the trade show?"*

Here Juanita matches by describing the decision point, then inviting Javier to recommend a choice, thereby making a decision to let go and move on.

Juanita could fall into the trap that many well-intentioned and inexperienced managers do: give advice and direct the next steps. How often are you presented with information from a peer or subordinate, and your immediate response is to give advice or draw a conclusion when nobody has asked you for that? How often do you jump the gun and preempt thoughtful and accountable thinking from the other person? I do it every day! And here's my distorted rationale: as a leader it's my job to make the call, share my conclusions, weigh in and take charge. This is distorted not because I shouldn't do these things under any circumstances. It's distorted because my job is to help my people increase their capability at Resourcefulness.

Ownership over decisions and choices is a tremendously powerful thing. Taking away that authority and accountability from someone should be done as rarely as possible, only in extreme situations, and only with a clear conversation about why. Otherwise, inviting the Choice to Move out of Resourcefulness by making a decision and letting go is the best thing a leader can do to facilitate accountability.

Javier is faced with a choice. Which of the three ads should he choose for the trade show? To answer this question will require him to take the risk to let go of the possibilities associated with the other two ads and put his judgment on the line. By posing this question to Javier, Juanita as the leader, has asked more from him. She's asked him to move beyond analysis and problem-solving and into a mode of behavior and accountability. Some people embrace this risk and responsibility. Some recoil and avoid because they are afraid of many things associated with the choice, such as resistance, avoidance, or rejection from the other person. Without making the choice, the next level of performance isn't possible.

The response to the invitation to move is rarely a simple "Sure, I'll do that." Even when someone is willing to move, they may say, "Not yet." Javier may want clarification about the choice. He may feel very uncomfortable about making the choice at this time, perhaps because he is waiting for some critical information to come in. Javier may be willing to recommend the best ad, and isn't yet prepared to do that. In these cases, a process of negotiation can facilitate the Choice to Let Go and Move On.

Javier could respond like this: "Juanita, I will be ready to make a recommendation tomorrow. We have one more set of analytics to run." Juanita can decide to push forward with her original invitation by saying, "I want your decision today. Will you do this, based on the information you currently have?" Or, she could negotiate and refine her invitation by saying, "Sure, what time tomorrow can I count on your decision?"

Matching at Resourceful can take many forms, all of them with the purpose of clarifying what decisions need to be made in order to translate knowledge into action. Here are some common ways of expressing this principle:

> *"We've seen the pros and cons. Which one will we choose?"*

> *"The consultant has given us recommendations. Which ones will we implement?"*

> *"We've researched the situation and understand our options. What course of action will we take now?"*

Skilled leaders, mentors, coaches, and facilitators are able to synthesize the resources that have been collected at Resourceful and point an individual or group toward the key decisions to be made. Avoiding the choice to move beyond Resourceful will often lead people to either get stuck (analysis paralysis) or go to Rescuer (start giving advice on what others should do).

Making the choice to Let Go and Move On can happen around a big issue, such as finalizing a new company brand image, or on a small scale such as taking a consultant's advice that the new brand should be more customer-friendly and directing the marketing department to develop concepts around that theme. Negotiators understand that making the choice to Let Go and Move On around small decisions can help build confidence to make bigger decisions later on. If you are trying to Match and Move someone out of Resourceful and are encountering resistance, try breaking the big decision into smaller ones.

Salespeople strive to never end a conversation without some commitment to action, no matter how small. They know that unless and until a person makes the choice to Let Go and Move On, a successful sale is still beyond their reach.

Maybe Javier won't recommend which ad to use. However, he might be willing to start by narrowing it down to the top two. Juanita can help Javier make small decisions along the way to bigger and more scary decisions. He might then be willing to forecast the benefits and consequences of either choice.

This action step, in turn, might get him to the point where he is willing to make the ultimate call.

When people are resisting the invitation to move out of Resourceful, here are some questions that can help identify and isolate the problem:

> *"What information do you still need in order to make the decision? Is it reasonable to believe that you can obtain it?"*

> *"Will knowing more make the decision any easier? How?"*

> *"What are you most worried about regarding this decision?"*

> *"If you make the choice, what consequences do you anticipate? How will you deal with those consequences?"*

For the choices that matter most, we can't guarantee no negative consequences. There's never a way to avoid all fear and loss. This is OK. Leading out of drama requires leaders to acknowledge this, give space to talk about it, help people process it, and move forward anyway. Compassionate accountability is about walking into the fire, together.

Ultimately, making the choice to Let Go and Move On involves taking personal responsibility for a choice and a course of action associated with that choice. It's all about obtaining a commitment, a contract to carry out an action or series of actions. Unless someone has made a commitment to a course of action that involves higher levels of accountability and risk, they have not moved beyond Resourcefulness.

Here are some Resourcefulness Match phrases that may come in handy as you develop and practice your own repertoire:

> *"You've put a lot of thought into that."*

> *"I can tell you've considered the options."*

> *"It sounds like you understand the options."*

> *"What's next?"*

And, some additional invitations to make the Choice to Let Go and Move On.

"Which option will you choose?"

"What is your decision to go forward?"

"What will you lose by making this decision?"

"What behavioral commitments are you willing to make?"

"What action are you willing to take?"

MATCH AND MOVE FROM PERSISTENT TO OPEN: INVITING THE CHOICE TO STOP AND LISTEN

Commitments and contracts are meant to be followed through. Persistence is about finishing what you start, doing what you said you would do, and sticking to your non-negotiable boundaries and commitments. Without it, we wouldn't be able to count on people and there would be no consistency in our lives.

Persistence is highly effective to a point. Overused or abused, Persistence becomes legalism, closed-mindedness and tunnel vision. In many companies, people are afraid to make commitments because they are a potential death sentence—a promise to plunge into action with no opportunity to reevaluate, make a mistake, or adjust the plan. The problem with Persistence is that it's not Open. To avoid getting stuck and keep the cycle moving in a healthy direction requires a choice to Stop and Listen. In the previous chapter we covered in detail how to apply this principle to ourselves. How do we invite others to move out of Persistence towards Openness by making the choice to Stop and Listen?

Juanita ended her day with a short team meeting with the three project managers most involved in the upcoming trade show. To her surprise and satisfaction, Javier came in with a recommendation on which ad to use. Mary, who was in charge of getting all the print collateral ready, seemed frustrated. She reiterated her promise to have samples of all the materials ready for the team to review next week, but was concerned that the printer, Color Corp, wouldn't be able to deliver on time.

Juanita knew that Compassion Corp's relationship with Color Corp hadn't always been the smoothest. Color Corp had worked with three different representatives from Compassion Corp in the last year, and there was often confusion about deliverables and responsibilities. Juanita stepped up to the opportunity to Match and Move.

> *"Mary, I sure do appreciate your commitment to this project. Yes, we do need to meet our deadlines so the team can review the collateral before it goes to production. How is your relationship with Color Corp?"*

Matching Persistence is about acknowledging and resonating with relevant commitments, boundaries, and non-negotiables. Moving is about stopping the task focus long enough to check in with oneself and others to see what else might be going on. In this situation, Juanita had a hunch that continuing to push for accountability and follow through wasn't likely to be effective. She invited Mary to step back and take stock, get some distance from the non-negotiables and deliverables long enough to see what else might be going on. In this case, the key was to re-focus on relationship issues, feelings, motives, and connection.

Mary accepted the invitation by responding,

> *"I have been stressed. It's important to me to meet these deadlines and I don't have control over Color Corp's priorities. Continuing to remind them isn't working because I seem to be getting more and more mistakes from them. This only pushes things back further. I don't feel like we are on the same wavelength much of the time."*

By making the choice to Stop and Listen, Mary recognized some very important factors that could have a significant impact on her ability to be effective in her role. Next, Mary went to Open and disclosed her concerns, as well as her desire to build a strong, trusting relationship with Color Corp because they had a history of doing solid work for Compassion Corps. She went on to ask for help from the group (Choice to State Your Wants), which led to a productive team discussion about next steps (Resourcefulness). Mary decided to make a personal visit to Color Corp (Choice to Let Go and Move On) and committed to report back to the team by the following Monday (Persistence).

Juanita's Match and Move with Mary ignited an entire trip around the Compassion Cycle, involved the team, and brought them to a much more productive place, all in a matter of minutes.

COACHING ACCOUNTABILITY WHEN THERE'S NO DRAMA

Failure to Stop and Listen leads to countless strained relationships, health problems, failed change initiatives, and over-budget projects. What has it cost you?

People aren't always as receptive as Mary. Sometimes they are so immersed in their own priorities and needs that they are unable or unwilling to Stop and Listen. In this case, the Persistence Match may take a different form. Let's suppose that Mary didn't accept the invitation, denied any problems, and reiterated her intention to keep reminding Color Corp about their commitments and deadlines. Juanita may have tried something like this;

> *"Mary, I value our relationship with Color Corp and am committed to making sure it stays strong. I don't believe that continuing to push them will help. You seem frustrated and they are making mistakes. Will you step back and consider what else might be going on?"*

This version of Match and Move is firmer, more explicit, and shows us that Mary's behavior is bumping up against one of Juanita's non-negotiables (maintaining a strong relationship with Color Corp). There is no drama—not yet. If Mary goes into drama instead of accepting the invitation (e.g., insults Color Corp for being incompetent), or if Juanita experiences a significant gap between what she wants and what she's experiencing from Mary, she can choose to use the next tool in her tool belt, the Formula For Compassionate Conflict.

Here are some Persistence Match phrases that may come in handy as you develop and practice your own repertoire:

> *"Thanks for your commitment."*

> *"I know this is important to you."*

> *"You've been working really hard on this."*

> *"I know I can trust you."*

> *"Keep trucking!"*

> *"We'll see this through together."*

"I've got your back."

"You can count on me."

And, some additional invitations to make the Choice to Stop and Listen.

"You've been pushing really hard. How are YOU doing?"

"How is your body handling this stress?"

"What's your gut telling you?"

"How are your people handling the added pressure?"

"Is there anything they may want to tell you, if you asked?"

"The project is important, and so are you. How's it going?"

UP, DOWN, OR SIDEWAYS!

Match and Move may seem like something only leaders could do with their subordinates, right? False! Match and Move is about compassionate account-ability, not about power or position. Anyone can use this with a peer, superior, or subordinate. It can be used with a spouse, a parent, or a child. The difficulty isn't in the position or power differential. The challenge lies in engaging in positive conflict and staying out of drama.

Ask one hundred people with whom they would have the most difficulty engaging in positive conflict. Some will point to their superiors because, "I could never confront my boss. That would be suicide." Some say subordi-nates because, "I don't want them to think I don't like them or make them afraid of me." Others say they struggle most with peers because, "That would be awkward and I don't want to ruin our friendship." Still others say family members because "They have so many expectations of me." Each one of these reasons is contaminated by one of the four Myths. I'm not saying it will be easy. I am arguing that Match and Move comes from a place of "I'm OK. You're OK," so it doesn't perpetuate myths.

Juanita used Match and Move to "lead down" (from a position of greater power) with a subordinate. Here are some examples of using Match and Move to "lead sideways" (from a position of equality) with a peer. Can you diagnose the Compassion Match and the Choice to Move invitation?

> *"Sounds like you have really researched your options. Which school are you going to choose?"*

> *"I agree that having an open relationship with your husband is important. How does he feel about it?"*

> *"I'm really sorry you were fired. Anything I can do to help?"*

Using Match and Move to "lead up" to a superior might look like this;

> *"That's great news! I'm excited about your promotion. If there's anything I can do to help, will you let me know?"*

> *"I have two important projects I'm working on for you. Which one do you want me to focus on first?"*

> *"I've been giving you status reports each Monday like you asked. How are you feeling about it so far?"*

Match and Move is a great coaching tool to enhance positive accountability with anyone in your life. When you are ready to learn about our strategy for full-on compassionate conflict, turn the page.

Want to enhance your learning experience?
- Consult the Personal Development Guide in Appendix A, along with your Drama Resilience Assessment profile.

TEN

The Formula for Compassionate Conflict

CONFRONTING DRAMA WITH
COMPASSIONATE ACCOUNTABILITY

You've come this far. You've recognized your own drama tendencies, diagnosed the drama around you, and made some decisions to change your behavior. You've practiced strategies to be more Open, Resourceful, and Persistent. You are trying to be more diligent about following the rules of the Compassion Cycle and make decisions to move from point to point on the cycle. You've even been helpful in coaching some of your key players to step up their level of accountability. If you are doing any of these things, you're helping to reduce the casualties typically associated with negative conflict. You are armed with the building blocks of positive conflict.

Are you ready to take on the beast?

CASE STUDY: DO YOU KNOW CFO SAM?

I can still remember when Jamie Remsberg, my co-founder, co-owner, business partner and trainer extraordinaire, told me about the first time she used the formula for compassionate conflict with someone in a training environment. It was epic, at least for us trainers who face full-on drama every day in our professional work. Jamie is one of the most gifted, level-headed, compassionate, and strong people I know. She can handle just about anything. She has a magical way of de-escalating situations, gaining buy-in, and creating environments where people behave themselves and grow.

On this particular day, about three years ago, Jamie was facing our toughest challenge. It was Day Two of a three-day intensive leadership communications training with the executive team of a large hospital. For the most part, the participants were great. They were curious, eager, and willing to challenge themselves to learn. Everyone, that is, but the Chief Financial Officer. We'll call him Sam. Sam came in swinging and never let up. He was hell-bent on sabotaging the training, proving Jamie wrong, and avoiding any accountability for his behavior. Comments like, "This doesn't seem relevant," or "Do you really expect us to buy into this?" revealed his intentions. If you are a trainer, board chair, or team leader, you've met Sam. Sam was opinionated, self-righteous, judgmental, manipulative, and suspicious. He questioned everything, interrupted, and criticized.

Jamie kept her cool and used her tools. She adapted her communication to match his personality, offered him positive psychological motivators and affirmations, and redirected him over and over. She encouraged other team members to speak up when it was clear that they'd had enough as well. Nothing worked.

Mere mortals would have thrown Sam out or thrown in the towel. I've seen trainers get eaten alive by these types, just like Cruella de Vil ate us alive on the company retreat. Seminars degenerate and become toxic, people shut down, and the whole situation spirals out of control. In high-stakes situations like this, there are a variety of options that Jamie could have chosen, all of them suicide. Giving in and playing the Victim role would have crushed her credibility as a trainer. Giving Sam unsolicited advice from the Rescuer position would have only escalated his defensiveness. Giving ultimatums and adopting a Persecutor position could easily have backfired if Jamie couldn't rally the power and authority to follow through.

Even without going into drama, Jamie could have continued to be compassionate, kind, and patient. The problem with this approach is that it would not have stopped Sam's disruptive, persecuting behavior, which was undermining learning for everyone. She could have brought the hammer down and ordered him to leave, yet this may have alienated him further and promoted a coup. Drama adversaries do not go away without a fight.

So Jamie decided to pull out her secret weapon, a tool we'd only lab-tested up to that point (which includes trying it out on our spouses and children). She looked Sam straight in the eye, mustered her most authoritative tone of voice, and said:

"I'm feeling angry about our interactions because I am working hard to teach this course to a group of people who want to learn and I don't feel this is your goal. I want to be effective as a trainer and also maintain a safe learning environment. I am willing to address your questions and concerns stated in a respectful way and support your learning. I am not willing to struggle against you. My number one commitment and responsibility is to facilitate a safe, curious, and consistent learning environment for everyone. Going forward, will you please discontinue all criticism and negative comments? If you are unable to do this, you may leave. How does this sit with you?"

Sam stopped dead in his tracks. He was silent for what seemed like minutes, while everyone in the room held their breath. Finally, he spoke. "I'm sorry," Sam told the group, "I will comply with Jamie's requests and participate more positively."

After the training, one participant privately asked Jamie, "What type of voodoo magic did you work on Sam?" Another said, "I've never seen anyone stand up to him in that way, and never seen him back down like that." That was the first documented use of our formula for Compassionate Conflict in a public setting!

CASE STUDY: DO YOU KNOW FARMER SAM?

The first time I tried the formula in public was with a church group. I was facilitating a congregation-wide training and strategy session around how to improve outreach, grow the congregation, and become more relevant to younger generations. We were wrapping up a three-hour session with about 150 people, and the only thing left to do was to decide on a date for our next meeting.

Several dates were suggested and one seemed to be the best for nearly everyone, so we put it to a congregational vote. Everyone was sitting around tables in the fellowship hall while I stood up to count the votes. We were trying a new decision-making process for this vote called the Thumbometer. It's a method of voting in which people cast either a thumbs up (full support), thumbs sideways (compliance with a commitment not to sabotage), and thumbs down (opposition with a commitment to more discussion). When it came time to vote, 149 people voted thumbs up. No one voted sideways. And one person voted thumbs down.

This wasn't just any person. This was Farmer Sam, a tall, lanky, 70-year-old farmer with leathery brown skin and a scowl that could clear out a committee meeting in a hurry. He didn't just vote thumbs down. He stood up, stuck his arm as far out as he could, and thrust his weathered, calloused thumb downward with such vigor that I could hear a groan ripple through the congregation. I heard someone near me whisper, "Here we go! Watch out!"

I must have been naive or delusional because I decided this was the perfect time to try the Formula for Compassionate Conflict—for the first time. I was standing across the room from Farmer Sam and began walking toward him. Speaking in whispers, several congregants urged me not to do whatever they thought I was going to do. I guessed there must have been some casualties in this church's past, and they probably involved Sam. Sam folded his arms and stared right at me, as if to say, "Now what are you going to do, huh!?"

Here's what I said:

"Sam, I care about your perspective and I want to hear what's behind your vote. If you have questions or something you'd like to talk about, we're here to listen. Your thumbs-down vote comes with a commitment to further conversation. Where are you at on this?"

Sam looked at me in disbelief. "That date won't work for me," he said gruffly. "Can't do it."

Another groan rippled throughout the room. In retrospect, I think well-meaning people may have been trying to tell me to back away and run for cover. Instead, I persisted:

"Sam, I am sorry this date won't work for you. I care about your input and participation in this process because you are an important part of the group. What alternatives would you suggest? We aren't leaving until we have a date that works for you and the others. I'm listening."

Sam's crusty demeanor started to soften. He slowly pulled his datebook out of his checkered shirt pocket. He opened it to the month of July and I saw big green highlighted lines stretching through several dates on his calendar, including the date on which we were voting. He pointed to the line and said in a near-whisper: "I am harvesting that day and I really don't want to miss our next session. I know it works for everyone else, but I can't make it."

I'm not sure if anyone else heard what Sam said, but it didn't matter. I asked Sam if he'd like to suggest a different date and he pointed to a Saturday afternoon two weeks later. I asked Sam if we could put this new date to a vote and he agreed. I've never seen so many thumbs thrust so far up in the air. This time the sound was one of relieved laughter.

After the meeting, Sam told me, "Thank you for sticking with me through that. I'm so glad we found a date that allowed me to join the group. I didn't want to miss it because I believe it is worthwhile." Many members of the church approached me afterwards with reactions that were similar to what Jamie received in her training with the hospital executive team.

How often has one toxic person held your entire team or organization hostage with their drama behavior? Has this become a pattern? Does everyone play along and perpetuate the drama? The two examples above show what's possible when we confront drama with compassionate accountability. These two situations have turned into thousands over the past three years, changing how leaders do everything from running team meetings to giving performance reviews to supporting the resolution of highly stressful board member conflicts.

THE FORMULA FOR COMPASSIONATE CONFLICT

What did Jamie do with CFO Sam? What did I do with Farmer Sam? What did Juanita do with Sally? What did CEO Dan do with his team member who wouldn't sign the compensation agreement? We all used the formula to respond to a drama role. The Formula for Compassionate Conflict is affectionately known as O-R-P-O. Sing it to the tune of the old Oreo commercials for more impact!

$$CC = O \blacktriangleright R \blacktriangleright P \blacktriangleright O$$

Compassionate conflict can work very well by using a series of compassion statements strung together, in the order shown above: Open, Resourceful, Persistent, and finishing up with Open. We've discovered this formula through a lot of practice, trial and error, research, and simulations. This formula is a big improvement over the one in my previous book, *Beyond Drama*. We encountered some problems with that method because it invited some people to lose focus on themselves and blame others, as well as give ultimatums. This was not our intention, and it motivated us to do better. We have evolved our understanding of compassionate conflict considerably over the last few years.

The Formula can be used any time you detect a drama role in yourself or another person, or you identify a significant gap between what you want and what you are experiencing and want to pursue a solution that requires conflict. Here's how it works:

Start at Open. Begin by disclosing your own feelings relevant to the situation, without giving in. If there's a gap between what you want and what you are experiencing, describe how you feel about that gap and how you want to feel instead. This is not the time to point out others' problematic behaviors or describe what people did or didn't do. It's all about identifying the core emotional responses you are having and figuring out how you'd prefer to feel instead.

Move to Resourceful. Describe any resources you are willing to offer to problem-solve how you will try to close the gap between what you want and what you are experiencing. If there is information or resources you want, describe what they are. Avoid giving advice or suggesting what others could or should do to help you. If you are addressing a "gap," this can be a perfect time to describe it—again, focusing on your own reactions and reflections. Jamie did this with Sam, explaining that she had been ineffective in her training so far and was losing time with the group.

Progress to Persistent. State your boundaries or "non-negotiables," as well as your commitments. What is the situation really about for you? What's at stake? What are you willing or unwilling to do? Avoid ultimatums. It's tempting to make threats to, or demands of, another person and lose focus on your own behavior and choices.

Finish with Open. Return to Open by checking in with yourself or others about their perspective, feelings, and desires. Stop to listen and be receptive. Conflict is difficult, and by this point in the formula, the other person has received a strong dose of positive conflict. It's appropriate and necessary to allow them to experience and respond.

Complete all four steps in order, starting and ending with Open. By doing so, you will follow all three Rules of the Compassion Cycle. Let's analyze how Juanita, Jamie, and I used the formula.

	Juanita with Sally	Jamie with CFO Sam	Nate with Farmer Sam
Open	I am uncomfortable with this conversation because I want be helpful and support you in feeling confident.	I'm feeling angry about our interactions because I am working hard to teach this course to a group of people who want to learn and I don't feel this is your goal. I want to be effective as a trainer and also maintain a safe learning environment.	Sam, I care about your perspective and I want to hear what's behind your vote.

	Juanita with Sally	Jamie with CFO Sam	Nate with Farmer Sam
Resourceful	I am willing to support you in problem-solving how to get what you want.	I am willing to address your questions and concerns stated in a respectful way and support your learning.	If you have questions or something you'd like to talk about, we're here to listen.
Persistent	I am not willing to criticize Fred or continue to hear you complain about your situation and put yourself down.	I am not willing to struggle against you. My number one commitment and responsibility is to facilitate a safe, curious, and consistent learning environment for everyone. Going forward, will you please discontinue all criticism and negative comments. If you are unable to do this, you may leave.	Your thumbs down vote comes with a commitment to further conversation.
Open	I care about you.	How does this sit with you?	Where are you at on this?

Here are a few more examples of the formula in action. Can you pick the O-R-P-O transition in each one?

"I am concerned about our relationship going forward. I am curious how your promotion will change the way we relate to each other. I will respect your new boundaries. Where are you at with this?"

"I feel angry about what happened and want to clear the air. Will you make time to talk this through? I am really sorry for what I did and I want to make it right. What's your perspective?"

"I can relate to your anxiety. I feel like that a lot during tax season. I received great mentoring on this and would be happy to share what I've learned. Ultimately, I'm committed to whatever it takes for us to serve the client and keep from going crazy. I care about you."

"It is perfectly OK to feel that way. What has worked for you in the past in situations like this? The deadline is approaching and you can count on me to support you through this. I'm here for you."

Once you've identified the compassion skills within each statement, try an even more finely-focused analysis. See if you can pick out which of the three strategies is being used at each step of the way. Reference the three strategies for each compassion skill shown below. For example, in the first ORPO statement, the phrase, *"I am concerned about our relationship going forward"* is Open, and the strategy being used is Disclosure. In the last statement, the phrase, *"I am really sorry for what I did and want to make it right"* is an example of Persistence with the strategy of Accepting Responsibility. Practice your skills by coding the rest of the statements.

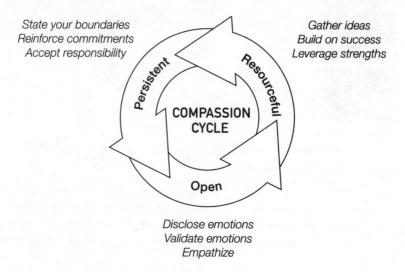

State your boundaries
Reinforce commitments
Accept responsibility

Gather ideas
Build on success
Leverage strengths

Persistent

Resourceful

COMPASSION
CYCLE

Open

Disclose emotions
Validate emotions
Empathize

MY PERSONAL ORPO STATEMENT

Is there a drama situation in your life that you'd like to address? Would you like to confront drama behavior with compassionate conflict? Try your hand at using the formula. Take a moment to write or type out what you would say. Whether you share it with that person or not, the formula is a powerful way to clarify what you have control over, what you are responsible for, and how you can approach the issue without drama.

Once you've written out your statement, practice saying it to yourself, out loud, all the way through. Repeat it several times until it flows. Share it with a trusted friend. How do you feel? What are you experiencing? How confident are you that you could share it directly with the person involved in the situation? Many of our clients spend a good deal of time journaling and practicing their formulas before ever engaging in conflict.

THE FORMULA FOR COMPASSIONATE CONFLICT 155

APPLYING THE FORMULA TO TYPICAL CONFLICTS

As a leader, you might frequently be faced with trying to calm down or support an employee who is worried or uncertain about pending changes. They may approach you with any drama role. For example; "I am freaking out about the merger. I don't know what to do (Victim—assuming a helpless position)."

Here's an ORPO that the supervisor could use to demonstrate her desire to "struggle with" the employee, while maintaining appropriate boundaries and accountability.

> "I can appreciate how scary this is (Open—Validate). I remember worrying about my job during our merger several years ago (Open—Empathize). What information can I provide that will help you (Resourceful—Gather Ideas)? I am committed to being transparent (Persistent—Follow through). I care about how you are doing (Open—Validate)."

What if you just got a promotion and you are nervous about what's involved? The gap you are experiencing is between your need to feel supported and adequately trained, and the uncertainty of the new job demands. You want to feel competent and confident. The gap is big enough that you decide to use ORPO to confront it with your boss.

> "I feel uncomfortable with this higher level of accountability because I anticipate conflict with my employees who were formerly peers (Open—Disclosure). I want training on how to negotiate these difficult conversations and you have a lot of experience in this area (Resourceful—Gathering Ideas and Leveraging Strengths). Will you commit to support me during this transition (Persistent—Reinforce Commitments)? I'd like to hear your perspective (Open—Validate)."

Here is another typical situation. A leader is uncertain about the level of cohesion amongst the team and wants to do whatever is possible to improve it. He or she might use ORPO like this:

> "I feel confused about the reactions I got from the team yesterday. I want us to be aligned (Open—Disclosure). I'm open to any feedback you want to share with me (Resourceful—Gather information). It is critical

for me to make any changes I can to improve our teamwork (Persistent
—Reinforce boundaries). *Where are you with this* (Open—Validate)*?"*

THE ORPO APOLOGY

You messed up. You did something wrong. What comes next can make it or
break it with your boss, employee, friend, or intimate partner. A good apology
takes humility, creativity, and skill. How you apologize can either turn things
back around, or make things worse. ORPO is terrific for apologies. It can help
everyone involved maintain their dignity and move towards creative problem-
solving. Use this template for making better apologies yourself, or coaching
others in the art of owning up and taking responsibility.

Step 1: Share Your Feelings (Open)

You messed up. You did something wrong. It doesn't feel good. The first step
is to identify and share how you feel about what you did. Are you embarrassed? Ashamed? Scared? Angry? Get honest. The person to whom you are
apologizing will respect your transparency. They don't want fake emotions or
false penitence—and they'll spot either one. They want to know your genuine
feelings. It may be awkward but it works. Hiding or distancing yourself from
your feelings gets you nowhere. Caution: Saying, "I'm sorry" doesn't count as
Open because it's more a statement of responsibility and ownership over the
behavior (Persistent) than it is a feeling.

Step 2: Identify Your Behavior and its Impact (Resourceful)

You messed up. You did something wrong. What did you do? Describe it.
No excuses, no rationalizations. Just describe it. Be specific. Unless you are
explicit about your behaviors, you are avoiding responsibility. If you don't
know what you did, find out from the other person. He or she wants to know
you understand what it is you are apologizing for. Vague statements like "I'm
sorry for whatever may have bothered you" are meaningless and disrespectful.
Statements like "I didn't call Johnson before Friday and you were left without
the information you needed" shows you own your behaviors and understand
the impact of those behaviors.

Step 3: Make it Right (Persistence)

You messed up. You did something wrong. Make it right. Making it right
shows that you can turn mistakes into stepping stones for success. This is the

time for a sincere apology. Apologies are not about feeling ashamed. They are about reaching out and moving forward. What are you willing to do to fix your mistake or wrongdoing? Maybe it involves simple behaviors you can control. Maybe it involves asking for help to learn something new. Maybe it involves changing your attitude and approach to problems in your life. Don't speak of general or far-in-the-future changes. Instead, suggest behaviors you are willing to implement today to begin to improve the situation. Focus only on your own behavior change, not changes you may want the other person to make.

Step 4: Be Receptive (Open)

It's great that you've come this far. A sincere and specific apology means that you're trying to rebuild a relationship with someone else. So this is the time to stop and let them respond. Are they satisfied with what you've offered? What do they need and want to make things right? Stop and listen.

Here are a couple examples of this four-step process in action.

"I feel embarrassed (Step 1: Open), because I forwarded the minutes to people who were not part of the executive team and by doing this I disclosed information that was not supposed to go beyond this group (Step 2: Resourceful). I am sorry. I'm willing to personally contact each person and let them know what I did and ask them to delete this message (Step 3: Persistent). How do you feel about this (Step 4: Open)?"

"I feel angry (Step 1: Open) that I missed the sales meeting this week because I know how important this is for our team performance (Step 2: Resourceful). I apologize. I'll review the minutes and check in with you to make sure I am up to speed on what I missed (Step 3: Persistent). I'm open to your perspective (Step 4: Open)."

Imagine the possibilities for customer service, team alignment, and morale! Applying The Formula to an apology helps us recognize why it can be counterproductive to force someone to apologize right away when they do something wrong. Coaching a child or adult through an effective apology can be improved dramatically by using this template to guide how you focus your energies. Here are some guiding questions to use when helping another person move toward an apology or help you develop your own apologies.

Openness Questions
- How do you feel about what happened?

- Without talking about anyone else, what emotions are you experiencing right now?
- What is your body telling you?

Resourcefulness Questions
- What did you do that caused harm or damage?
- What specific behaviors or choices did you make that contributed to a problem?
- What impact did your behaviors or choices have on others?

Persistence Questions
- What do you want to say to the person who is upset that will show you are serious about making it right?
- What could you do to help correct what happened or make it right?
- What principles or non-negotiables are at stake here?

WHY DOES THE FORMULA WORK SO WELL?

The Formula for Compassionate Conflict works so well because it complies with the rules of the Compassion Cycle. By starting at Open, it promotes an environment of safety where real feelings and motives can be revealed. I've had leaders challenge me on this, arguing that being Open when going into conflict is tantamount to professional suicide. Others point out that at the very least, Openness in the face of conflict would make others uncomfortable. While I can understand these concerns, especially if you've spent your life protecting yourself and hiding your emotions, I haven't seen it play out in real life. The reason is that the Formula doesn't stop at Open. It keeps moving, adding the problem-solving curiosity of Resourceful and the character strength of Persistent.

The Formula recognizes that no single compassion skill can adequately engage in positive conflict without the support of the others. Openness only has bite if it dedicates resources to learning at Resourceful and is clear about what's at stake at Persistence. Resourcefulness only thrives if it is informed by the true emotional motives at Open, and held accountable by the non-negotiables of Persistent. Persistence only has credibility if it has done its due diligence at Resourceful, and cares enough to continue along the cycle to Open, where it stops and listens.

The Formula offers multiple "points of entry" onto the Compassion Cycle. This is powerfully disarming and can be transformative for someone who's looking for drama. A person in drama can join you anywhere on the Compassion Cycle, wherever is the closest point to their true, best nature. Let's revisit the ORPO introduced earlier, where the boss asks his team for their input:

"I feel confused about the reactions I got from the team yesterday. I want us to be aligned (Open—Disclosure). I'm open to any feedback you want to share with me (Resourceful—Gather information). It is critical for me to make any changes I can to improve our teamwork (Persistent—Reinforce boundaries). I'd like to know where you are with this (Open—Validate)."

In this situation, people to whom the boss is speaking can join him anywhere on the Compassion Cycle. One person may be moved by his vulnerability and join at Open with empathy, saying, "I was confused as well. You aren't alone."

Another person may have some feedback to share. Given her boss's genuine invitation into Resourcefulness, she might say, "My sense was you asked a lot of questions and didn't give us time to answer. I think we could give you better input if you gave us advance warning on the questions."

A third person might accept the invitation into Persistence with a statement like, "I appreciate your commitment to teamwork. It's a foundational principle for our company."

Because it offers multiple points of entry onto the Compassion Cycle, the Formula sets the stage for healthy dialogue around what's most important.

HOW MANY TIMES DOES IT TAKE?

There's no guarantee that ORPO will work on the first try. It's hard for people in drama to receive a response that refuses to justify their respective ally or adversary motives, but ORPO invites them to take healthy personal responsibility to struggle "with" you instead of against you. This realization can invite a lot of uncomfortable responses from people. Embarrassment, defensiveness, vulnerability, fear, and anxiety are just a few. Couple that with the strong emotions associated with drama, and the tension can be extremely high. Most often, a person in drama will not accept your invitation the first time—maybe not even the second or third time. Struggling with someone may require a lot perseverance and patience. Staying out of drama yourself may be the best you can hope for, and that's a victory.

Several years ago we were in the middle of a leadership communication training program for a statewide service agency preparing to implement a new strategic plan. In the course of our relationship with this client, it became apparent that several participants were quite invested in undermining the success of the initiative. In one situation, we naively allowed one person to communicate privately with us through e-mail and text, ostensibly to process some struggles she was having in the communication training program. As it turned out, this person had a history of triangulating, and she used her "secret" relationship with us to manipulate organizational leadership. We had engaged in victim helping and magnified a problem that was already difficult for the CEO. We ended up in the line of fire because of our mistake.

The CEO was extremely angry with us, and for good reason. "Quite frankly, I don't know if we can trust you anymore," he shared with me. We realized that unless we could struggle with each other instead of against each other, there was little hope for reconciliation. The relationship mattered immensely to us because I deeply respected the CEO. In addition, the organization was making great strides and a lot was at stake.

I called the CEO and asked him to meet me for coffee to talk. He was skeptical, saying he wasn't sure it mattered. I sensed that he had written us off and had already created an ultimatum in his mind. So I sent him the following ORPO message: "I feel sad about where our relationship has gone because we want to be trustworthy and we care deeply about your company. I want to understand all I can about how you've experienced us and see if there's any way to rebuild our relationship. I am committed to sticking with this and making things right. What's your perspective?"

He agreed to meet for coffee. We met and talked for almost two hours. The first ORPO statement I used didn't magically fix anything. So I did it again, and again. Challenging as the situation was for both of us, we got through it. I tried a variety of strategies at each compassion skill—whatever seemed to be most appropriate for the situation. The CEO never disengaged and continued to disclose more and more information about the situation. His amazing tenacity, commitment to his team, and genuinely decent spirit kept him there. Finally—and I'll always remember this—he joined me at Open.

The CEO disclosed the embarrassment and loss of control he felt when members of his own executive team began to question his leadership. He shared his anger about our mistake and admitted that although he knew this wasn't our intention, it still hurt and had been festering for over a week. After he'd been Open, I was able to give a better apology that spoke to the real issue—an emotional motive I was unaware of until he shared it with me.

After that, the healing began. The CEO opened up to working on our relationship and even suggested some action steps we could take to help heal broken trust. Both of us had a much better idea of what we needed to do to move forward. We struggled together.

It was a six-month journey to get our relationship back on track. Our team recognized we had engaged in victim helping and ended up in the line of fire by magnifying a situation that was already difficult for the CEO. It took us a while, and we were able to recover and learn through this by using the same tools we teach our clients. This experience will always be a reminder to me of ORPO's power to engage in positive conflict, rebuild trust, and struggle together to create something amazing. It's also a reminder of how difficult the struggle can be.

The Formula for Compassionate Conflict may not work the first time you use it. With humility, creativity, perseverance, and practice, though, this process can change how you approach every conflict-producing situation and transform the energy into positive results.

TIPS FOR ORPO SUCCESS

As you begin practicing the Formula for Compassionate Conflict, these tips will help increase your chance of success.

1. **Be drama-free yourself.** It's impossible to successfully use The Formula when you are in drama. Why? Because in drama your motive is to find other drama roles to justify your myths. Use the tools throughout this book and the template in the next chapter to take care of yourself first.

2. **Be aware.** Pay attention to what drama roles are being played by others, and what roles you are tempted to play in response. Simply naming it and being aware of it can help resist the pull. Take time to journal after the fact about what happened, what roles people played, what roles you played, and the outcome.

3. **Be realistic.** Some people may not want to, or be able to, join you because of ingrained habits or fear of accountability. When leaders ask us for help knowing when to fire someone, we often recommend coaching them on how to apply The Formula with the employee regarding the issue at hand. When we are confident that the leader is using The Formula accurately and consistently (usually assessed through real-time observation and role-play), and the employee is still not responding, it's time to make the call. Even then, we help our clients use The Formula to negotiate the departure.

4. **Be patient.** Recognize that it may take many repetitions of The Formula in various forms to achieve success. First off, people may not trust your

motives if they aren't used to you being out of drama. That's OK. It's also OK to let them know what you are trying to accomplish. Imagine this ORPO: "I'm anxious because I am trying a new method to have healthy conflict. If you have any questions about what I am doing, I am happy to share. I am committed to staying out of drama even while we have difficult conversations. How does that sit with you?"

5. **Be prepared.** You probably won't successfully execute The Formula on your first try in the heat of battle. It may take five, ten, or sixty times before the other person joins you. That's OK! Being prepared means having a bank of options at O, R, and P to draw from. The next chapter will walk you through the process of preparing for conflict without casualties by having your bank of options beforehand.

6. **Be kind.** Realize that drama is just a role, not the real person behind the role. Responding to drama with ORPO sends a clear message to yourself and others that you will not participate in behavior that undermines another person's dignity and worth. Remember that the Compassion Cycle affirms the core beliefs that both you and I are worthwhile, capable, and accountable.

The Formula for Compassionate Conflict is a powerful tool. As you practice you will learn what works best and what doesn't work at all. You will find patterns in the types of ORPO statements you share as you discover what kinds of emotions, resources, and non-negotiable boundaries are most relevant to you. If at first you don't succeed, take heart. Try again and check back on the resources throughout this book to evaluate and improve your efforts. Did you use one of the three strategies for each Compassion Skill? Did you avoid Leading Indicators? Did you comply with the Rules of the Compassion Cycle? Did you let yourself get sucked into a drama role? The more you practice, reflect, and adjust, the better you will get!

The last chapter brings everything together to help you prepare to engage in conflict without casualties in your life. I'll share all of the tips and strategies we use with our clients to help them move out of drama and into compassionate accountability.

Want to enhance your learning experience?
- Consult the Personal Development Guide in Appendix A, along with your Drama Resilience Assessment profile.

ELEVEN

Conflict Without Casualties

PREPARING TO STRUGGLE WITH

Whatever the challenges ahead of you, preparation is one of the most important ways to ensure success. Positive conflict is no different in this regard. In this chapter I'll provide guidance on how to get and keep yourself healthy, and prepare to engage in positive conflict with minimal risk of casualties. Struggling with others to create something amazing is a tremendously rewarding journey.

STRESS-COPING HABITS AND SOLUTIONS

When stress hits, whether positive or negative, there are healthy and unhealthy ways of coping. Unhealthy coping may win you short-term relief, but it sets you up for drama in the long term. Here are some common unhealthy stress-coping habits that increase the chance of drama.

If You Stay, You Pay

In Chapter Four, I explored the importance of using the Compassion Skills wisely and the hazards of overusing them. When we're stressed, it's tempting to hunker down at our most developed compassion skill. It feels safer to stay there, and we feel more confident about what to do. But in order to cope with stress in a healthy way, we need resilience and flexibility, which can only be achieved by accessing all three Compassion Skills. Staying at one skill violates at least two rules of the Compassion Cycle. First, movement is necessary. Second, the only way forward is forward. Healthy stress-coping requires the Openness to recognize your feelings and the gaps between what you want and what you're experiencing. You need Resourcefulness to mobilize solutions, and Persistence to persevere and stay grounded.

The Solution: Keep moving forward, even if it's hard. Cultivate all three of your compassion skills so that you have a well-balanced toolkit for handling stress.

If You Skip, You Slip

Stress can be understood pretty simply by using this formula:

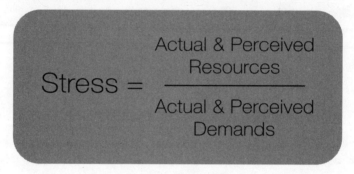

$$\text{Stress} = \frac{\text{Actual \& Perceived Resources}}{\text{Actual \& Perceived Demands}}$$

When the demands on us (both actual and perceived) outweigh the resources we have (or perceive to have), we experience stress. The more lopsided this equation becomes, the more likely this stress will spiral downward into distress. If a situation requires a resource that we don't have or is undeveloped, we can become stressed. We see this play out on the Compassion Cycle. What if I'm stranded on the side of a lightly traveled road with a flat tire, no cell-phone coverage, and nobody is coming by or stopping? Resourcefulness is probably the most significant skill required. In order to deal with the demands of the situation, I must change the tire by myself. If I don't know how to do that, I've got to figure it out. If I haven't developed Resourcefulness, I may skip it and go straight to Persistence, continuing to wait for a sympathetic motorist to happen by.

What if I've implemented a new policy regarding paid time off and my employees aren't complying as I expect? I've reinforced the policy through memos and the company newsletter (Persistent). In an attempt to gain compliance, I skip Open and go straight to Resourceful, trying another creative solution like slipping reminders into people's paychecks. Nothing changes. By skipping Open I've likely missed some very important information, namely the emotional experience and motives of employees in response to this policy. Taking time to stop and listen to them might provide insight into a more effective next step.

Skipping Open is one of the most common mistakes leaders make. They work hard at Resourceful to find solutions, implement them at Persistent then go about trying to influence compliance and buy-in. They mistakenly think that the key to success is being clear about, and reinforcing, expectations (Persistence), and communicating the change over and over (Resourceful). Most failed change initiatives happen because emotional motives and responses were never revealed, recognized, or affirmed.

The Solution: Discipline yourself to spend time at each Compassion Skill, in order. Review the Three Choices to Move and pay special attention to how you will recognize and respond positively when each choice presents itself to you.

RISK FACTORS FOR DRAMA AND HOW TO REDUCE THEM
There are certain factors, both under your control and beyond your control, that increase your risk for drama. Being aware of these and making necessary adjustments will help you stay healthy and resilient.

One-Trick Pony
We've all heard the saying, "If all you have is a hammer, then the whole world is a nail." During stress, it's tempting to resort to our most tried and true coping skills, the ones of which we're most confident. This is true for Compassion Skills. Relying on our most well-developed Compassion Skill to solve every problem is a significant risk factor for drama. Here are some examples of how this automatic response causes problems.

A highly dedicated and loyal team leader responds to every missed deadline by reiterating to his team the importance of being committed and not letting others down. By doing this, he inadvertently projects his own motivational needs onto his team members, invites them to feel as though they aren't measuring up, and suggests that Persistence is the only right way to be on time. He fails to see any other way to get from point A to point B.

A highly caring and supportive CEO approaches every conflict by bringing the parties together to talk it out, state positives about each other, and promise to be nice. Yet the behavior continues. She mistakenly believes that Openness can solve the complex problem of interdepartmental conflict. She fails to get to the root of the problem (Resourceful) or enforce boundaries regarding appropriate behavior (Persistent).

A highly creative ad agency has an unending supply of great ideas for getting people to click on their client's company Facebook page. Yet their Facebook page has generated no sales in six months. The agency has lost sight of the bigger picture (Persistence) and is out of touch with their client's distress (Open) because they stay at Resourceful. One day the client fires the ad agency. The agency has no idea why.

The Solution: Develop all your Compassion Skills, especially the ones in which you are weaker. Find friends, mentors, peers who are strong in a skill you want to work on. Observe them, interview them, and ask them for pointers and feedback.

The Speed of Change

Change happens. Faster and faster, it seems. Trying to keep pace is dizzying. Just as it gets harder and harder to hold on as the merry-go-round goes faster, the same is true for the Compassion Cycle. Vehicles going too fast around a corner are more likely to slip off into the ditch, especially if traction is compromised. People are more likely to slip off into the Drama Triangle if their complementary Compassion Skill is weak.

The Solution: There are several ways to deal with the speed of change. One way is to strengthen your Compassion Skills and choices to move. These will allow you to negotiate the bends more efficiently. Second, you can slow down and step back periodically. Resisting the speed of change requires perspective, the ability to recognize what change is important and necessary, and what change will serve no purpose other than to avoid feeling left out or inadequate. Change for change's sake can be crazy-making. Take stock of what changes you want to make, what external changes you really want to respond to, then do so with intentionality. Being intentional about change is critical to increase your sense of control and balance. By putting the Compassion Cycle together with the Three Choices to Move, we can generate a five-step process for negotiating change.

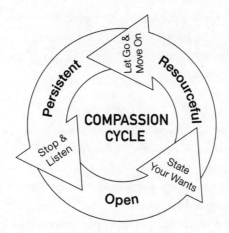

Step 1: Be Open
- How am I feeling about the change? How are you feeling?
- What am I experiencing as a result of the gap between what's going on and where I am? What are you experiencing?

Step 2: Make the Decision to State Your Wants
- What do I want instead? Don't focus on the behaviors or results from others, but rather an emotional end state you want that will feel comfortable and satisfying.
- What do you/we want instead?

Step 3: Be Resourceful
- What resources do I/you/we have access to that could help?
- What information or additional resources do I/you/we need to be successful?
- What success in my/your/our past could provide insight or energy to move forward?
- Who in my/your/our life might be able to help?
- What decisions do I/you/we need to make?

Step 4: Make the Decision to Let Go and Move On
- If I/you/we choose a particular course of action, what will be lost or given up?

- If I/you/we choose a particular course of action, what will be the consequences? Am I, or are we, willing to accept them?
- How will I/you/we authentically grieve the loss of options and security that comes with this change?

Step 5: Be Persistent
- What boundaries and principles are impacted by this change?
- What boundaries or principles will help me/you/us follow through on my/our decision?
- How will I/you/we keep going when obstacles are encountered, either internally or from the outside?
- Who will be my/your accountability partners, people who will help hold me/you accountable for goals and behaviors?

The Hostile Conspiracy

Drama invites drama and nature hates a vacuum. People in drama are continually recruiting allies and adversaries, so it can often feel like the whole world is out to get you when you try to choose compassion instead of drama.

The Solution: Awareness! The first step is awareness of yours and others' drama roles. Simply paying attention can go a long way in resisting the pull. Several of the tips for ORPO success in the previous chapter are also great guidelines for resisting the negative pull of drama from others.

Also, the more well-developed your compassion skills, the better chance you will have to generate a great ORPO response. Pay special attention to all three strategies for each compassion skill because each can come in handy depending on the situation. Finally, remember that behind most drama roles are latent or misused positive qualities. Refer back to Chapter 2 for a refresher. The most successful ORPO statements not only invite others out of drama, they invite them to bring their best selves to the table instead. Rejecting drama is great. Offering a healthy alternative is even better!

The Empty Bucket

It's nearly impossible to resist drama when our physical, emotional, psychological and spiritual defenses are down. Keeping yourself energized is a critical component of drama resilience.

The Solution: Fill your bucket. What energizes and affirms your best self? What types of activities and relationships are most fulfilling for you? Are you energized by being with friends? Do long walks fill your tank? How about sports, or massages, or time with your children? Figure it out then do these things as often as you can! I can't emphasize enough how important it is for you to take elegant care of yourself every day in order to engage in healthy conflict without casualties. If you aren't sure about what motivates you, there are several great assessment tools out there that can help.[1]

PREPARING FOR CONFLICT: BUILDING YOUR ORPO BANK

Before engaging in conflict, a little preparation can go a long way. Here is a template for gathering your thoughts, preparing to go multiple rounds of ORPO if necessary, and stay focused on your goals and intentions.

Step 1: Mind the Gap

It's easy to get sidetracked during conflict. The best-laid plans can be derailed in the blink of an eye. Minding the gap is about getting clear about what you are going to do and why. Here are a few questions to guide you:

- What is the most important issue you want to address?
- What behavior in yourself or another person most concerns you?
- What preconceived ideas or expectations do you have about this situation?
- Are you making any assumptions about yourself, another person, or the situation? What are they?
- How serious is the issue? What is the likelihood of drama?

Step 2: Build Your Open Bank

Strive to develop a robust list of options to choose from, including all three strategies:

Validate: Anticipate and be prepared to affirm the other person's feelings. This is a critical component because unless you are open to their experience, they will unlikely feel safe enough to struggle with you. What feelings might the other person(s) have and how will you validate them?

Empathize: Have you ever been in the other person's shoes? Do you have any similar experiences in your past? What was it like? How can you relate?

Disclose: Be prepared to disclose how you are feeling about the situation. Make a list of at least 3–4 feelings that are relevant.

Step 3: State Your Wants

What do you want? Don't focus on behaviors from the other person or how the world might act differently. Focus on your emotional motives. How do you want to feel differently? Getting clear about this will help you focus on what you can control, not on what others should or shouldn't do.

Step 4: Build Your Resourceful Bank

Before you enter into conflict, gather some resources. Prepare some statements and questions for each of the following Resourceful strategies that could apply to the situation.

Gather Ideas: Consider what information, relationships, and other resources you are willing to offer. What information do you need? Are you curious about the other person's motives or perceptions? Is there anything you should learn in order to be more effective? Refer to Chapter 2 about the hidden or misused strengths behind each drama role.

Build On Success: Have you solved similar conflicts successfully in the past? What successes do you or others involved in this conflict have that might inform how you handle this one?

Leverage Strengths: Focus on effort and strategies. How can you validate that someone is trying and has noble intentions, even if the output isn't what you want? How can you take advantage of their strengths?

Step 5: Choose to Let Go and Move on

Struggling with another person requires a decision to let go. Surrender the need to have it all figured out, the urge to get into drama and avoid responsibility, the impulse to back away and let someone else do the hard work, or assumptions you've made about yourself or another person. What will you have to let go of in order to be effective?

Step 6: Build Your Persistence Bank

Your Persistence bank will help you stay strong if the other person or group pushes your boundaries or asks you to compromise. To build your bank, fill in a few things at each one of these strategies.

State your boundaries: Get crystal clear what's at stake for you. What are your non-negotiables? What principles are at stake? Do you have obligations or duties to a third party that are motivating you to engage in conflict? Share and own those obligations. What are you willing to do to get what you want?

Reinforce non-negotiables: Are there rules that have been broken? Deadlines missed? Contracts or boundaries violated? If they are relevant to your conflict, write them down. This is not about blaming or giving ultimatums. It's about explicitly identifying any agreements or behavioral contracts that are relevant to the conflict.

Accept responsibility and make it right. Whether you are apologizing or simply owning up to your part of the conflict, it's critical that you share responsibility for both the conflict and the solution. Remember that there would be no conflict unless you wanted something you weren't getting. As crazy as it may seem, you have to own your part in the conflict by owning up to what you want. For what are you willing to take responsibility?

Step 7: Choose to Stop and Listen

Conflict is hard work. It's tempting to stop at Persistent, sit back, and expect the other person to give you want you want. Realize, however, that because conflict is a struggle, it inevitably takes a toll on our heart, body, mind, and spirit. It's OK and important to step back and make space to experience this. Listen to your own inner voice. Listen to the other person. It's only through this return to Open that two parties can increase their bond and commitment to compassion.

Step seven returns you to Open, ready to hear whatever the other person does next. They may join you in the Compassion Cycle, or they may continue in Drama. Either way, you are ready for what's next.

Appendix B provides a template for completing all steps in preparation for a positive conflict situation. Make copies of this template and use it for each conflict you encounter. Use what you write down to develop your ORPO statements when you apply the Formula for Compassionate Conflict.

DISCOVERING AND OWNING YOUR EMOTIONAL MOTIVES

Most people confuse disclosure with sharing information and opinions. I find it ironic and somewhat comical that people will often start a sentence with, "If I'm going to be perfectly honest," and go on to share an opinion about another person. They've done nothing to open themselves up. In this book I've argued that disclosure is about being Open about one's own emotions, not opinions, thoughts, plans, or even goals. These are more akin to Resourcefulness.

"Problems seldom exist at the level at which they are expressed. We do not see things as they are. We see things as we are."

—Anaïs Nin

Much negative conflict arises from failure to be aware of, and disclose, one's own emotional motives. Most, if not all, energy we expend is driven by emotional motives. An emotional motive is an emotion towards which you are driving. It is often ignited by its opposite emotion. When you are unhappy or unsatisfied, you can often discover what you really want by imagining the opposite of how you are currently feeling. For example, I'm anxious and I want to feel calm. I'm scared and I want to feel safe. I'm worried and I want to feel confident.

Managers may think they are motivated by clearly defined goals, but beneath the surface, they want to avoid a sense of loss. Executives may tell people their goal in researching every possible scenario is simply to cover their bases, but deep down they are afraid of being surprised or scared by their inability to protect the people for whom they are responsible. Team leaders may tell their teams that they just want to "work it out and get along," but inside they are angry because their personal boundaries have been crossed.

Leading self and others out of drama with compassionate accountability starts and ends with emotional responsibility. The Formula for Compassionate Conflict is bookended by Openness, so mastery of emotions is the cornerstone.

Dr. Taibi Kahler, an internationally acclaimed behavioral psychologist, has identified six core emotional motives that he calls "Phase Issues." Different personality types have unique issues that are especially difficult for them to handle well. Depending on personality architecture and phase of life, one of these six is primary. Persons who identify, disclose, and experience these emotional motives can engage in healthy problem-solving, transparent relationships, and effective resolution of problems. Anyone who masters this art can develop deeper levels of authenticity and intimacy in relationships.

Kahler's six phase issues are Fear, Loss, Anger, Responsibility, Autonomy, and Bonding/Intimacy. Avoiding or trying to hide these emotional motives is an invitation into drama. This is why drama-based problem-solving is so draining: energy is spent on symptom-management instead of the real issue. When you identify and disclose your emotional motive, you may feel vulnerable. But it also allows your community to be most helpful to you. Authenticity is one of the most powerful leadership qualities you can develop.

"You either walk inside your own story and own it, or you stand outside your story and hustle for your worthiness."
—Brené Brown

"The inner thought coming from the heart represents the real motives and desires. These are the cause of action."
—Raymond Holliwell

When life presents us with a difficult issue, the discomfort we feel is natural. Recognizing, disclosing, and owning the emotional motive beneath the surface leads to authentic, healthy problem-solving.

What follows are narratives around each of the six emotional motives. As you read these narratives, reflect on which one is most consistent with your experience.

Fear

"I am a natural protector."

It is my duty to protect my family, my company, my employees, and my constituency. Because of the unpredictable nature of the world, and of people, I can't always fulfill my duty perfectly. This is frightening. That's OK. If I recognize and disclose this fear, ask for help, and acknowledge that many of my behaviors are motivated by my desire to feel less afraid and more safe, then I can stay healthy. If I hide or cover up this emotional motive, my behaviors will likely include chronic suspicion, problems with trust, self-righteous arrogance, and pessimism.

Loss

"I'm a natural planner."

It is my duty to fix things, plan things out, and be sure that there are no surprises. Because of the unpredictable nature of the world, and of people, I lose control of life. Losing things (including time spent and opportunities) is sad. That's OK. If I recognize and disclose my sadness around the loss, ask for help, and acknowledge that many of my behaviors are motivated by the need to feel in control, then I can stay healthy. If I hide or cover up this emotional motive, my behaviors will likely include rigid micromanaging; obsessive and compulsive behavior around even the tiniest issues of time management, order-liness, and money; and a critical attitude around how lazy, irresponsible, and stupid everyone else is.

Anger

"I'm a natural caregiver."

It is my duty to show compassion, make sure everyone is happy, and promote harmony. Because of the nature of humanity, people do mean things, sometimes even on purpose. I feel angry about that. That's OK. If I recognize and disclose my anger around the way people treat me and each other, and acknowledge that many of my behaviors are motivated by the need to feel close to others again, then I can stay healthy. If I hide or cover up this emotional motive, my behaviors will likely include losing confidence and self-esteem, taking things too personally, and getting depressed because I've turned the anger on myself instead.

Responsibility

"I'm a natural 'funster.'"

It is my pleasure to enjoy life, play with others, and create new things. Because I make mistakes, and because the world wants to count on me, I experience the burden of expectations. I feel responsible, and that feels uncomfortable and restrictive. That's OK. If I recognize and disclose my feelings of responsibility to myself and my community, ask for help, and acknowledge that many of my behaviors are motivated by the need to freely express myself, then I can stay healthy. If I hide or cover up this emotional motive, my behaviors will likely include blaming, complaining, and sarcasm to avoid accepting responsibility for my behavior.

Bonding/Intimacy

"I'm a natural do-er."

I take great pride in my ability to make things happen and take care of business. Self-sufficiency is one of my best qualities. Because the world doesn't always move at my pace and people want to get close to me, I feel tied down. Being emotionally reliable and present with another person is very uncomfortable. That's OK. If I recognize and disclose my fear of intimacy, ask for help, and acknowledge that many of my behaviors are motivated by the need to avoid close relationships, then I can stay healthy. If I hide or cover up this emotional motive, my behaviors will likely include negative drama and manipulation in order to push people away and position myself as superior as a way to avoid feeling close.

Autonomy

"I am a natural dreamer."

I relish the vast wonder of my imaginative mind and freedom to spend time there. Because I have to get things done and because people often leave me alone, I feel the push to get out of my imagination, get into the real world, and make decisions. I feel very uncomfortable with this kind of autonomy. That's OK. If I recognize and disclose this discomfort with self-direction, ask for help, and acknowledge that many of my behaviors are motivated by my desire to avoid autonomy, then I can stay healthy. If I hide or cover up this emotional motive, my behaviors will likely include avoidance, isolation, and a sense of insignificance.

Which emotional motive resonates most with you? Is there more than one? What might be holding you back from deeper authenticity? What benefits could you gain from disclosing and honoring your emotional motives to be more authentic? How might knowing these motives help you empathize with others and struggle with them through conflict? What's stopping you?

SANDY'S STORY: COMPASSIONATE ACCOUNTABILITY THROUGH CRISIS

One of my business partners, Sandy, is an Energizer Bunny. Originally from Brazil, she has achieved tremendous success since moving to the U.S. more than 30 years ago. Among her many accomplishments, Sandy has directed the learning and development department for a large manufacturing company, led significant change initiatives for a Fortune 500 company, and raised a family. She can get more done in half a day than most of us can do in a week. Her skill set is vast, her energy is infectious, and Sandy has experienced her share of crisis.

Sandy is one of the Next Element owners and has been with the company since 2012. She tells anyone who asks that this is the hardest job she's ever had, and the most rewarding. Living and practicing compassionate accountability isn't for the faint of heart. Its principles and strategies have helped all of us navigate difficult situations. One in particular stands out for Sandy. I was so touched by her story that I asked if she'd be willing to share it in this book. She agreed, and I am grateful. For anyone going through a personal crisis, I hope this story not only lets you know you aren't alone, but it shows you what's possible when the principles of compassionate accountability and positive conflict are applied internally. These are Sandy's words:

> I have a great life, a great family, a great job. I feel fulfilled. I have great life skills. I am motivated by relationships and by getting things done. At Next Element, we are all about relationships and getting things done. So, this is a match made in heaven.

> These skills have saved my butt many times. I feel confident I can address any tough situation from an "I'm OK. You're OK." position. I am flying high!

> And then, something happened that turned my world upside down. You see, I have a 40-year-old son who is a single parent of two amazing kids. He is a great man and a great dad. And he suffers from epileptic seizures. Once every two or three years, I get a phone call from where he happens to be, saying he had one. When I get to him, he is sitting up, talking normal, even though he is exhausted. So, we talk, and life moves on.

Not this last time around....

I was in the office having a very productive meeting with my work family, talking about possibilities. I noticed I had a voicemail and quietly listened to it. At the same time, my husband walked in to the office. This was highly unusual since work is 30 minutes from my house. I looked at him while I heard his voice saying my son had a seizure and that we needed to get to the hospital right away. I felt confused.

So, we took off to the hospital. I found my son on the stretcher, covered with blood, with a neck brace, a nasty cut on the forehead (you could see his eye ducts), a broken nose, and who knows what else. Thankfully, he was lucid, although confused. So far, so good.

While we waited anxiously for the test results to come back to tell us whether or not Dave had a broken neck, a heart problem, or was on drugs, he had another nasty seizure. I'd never seen that before except on TV, and let me tell you, it was VERY different and a lot scarier!

I'll save you the gory details. We left the ER seven hours later, with lots of stitches, contusions, medication, and plenty of instructions on what to do and what not to do.

Fast forward a bit. The next couple of days were eventful and stressful. I took on my "mama bear" persona and took care of everything and everyone. I made sure my son took his meds, lined up doctors' appointments, the kids were fed, etc. I felt needed, and moved at one million miles an hour.

Once my son stabilized a bit, everything stopped. I found myself alone in my house, walking in circles, not knowing what to do or where to go. So I decided to take a warm bath. That always seems to do the trick for me when my spirits are down.

In the tub I hit bottom and cried. Crying just doesn't seem to describe it. I bawled. I yelled. I screamed. It was a cry of desperation. After a while, I had no more energy or tears to shed. So, I took a deep breath and decided to do something for myself.

I started at Open with small steps; feel the warmth of the water, listen to my favorite music, smell the relaxing salts, nurture my sensory needs. That felt good. For a little bit. And then I cried some more. And bawled. And screamed. This attempt to "fill my bucket" didn't last long. My distress was too deep, and I had to do something more to avoid falling into a desperate type of depression.

Here is where I can say things started to transform for me. I decided to apply the skills I learned, and do some major self-reflection. I decided to try using the Formula for Compassionate Conflict with myself. I reflected on the most important questions for using the Cycle.

How am I really feeling? What do I want? What will I do to get there? What will be my boundaries to ensure I don't fall back and quit on my planned approach? How will I know things are working?

So I took the steps, one by one:

I entered at Open: How was I really feeling? Scared. Because: I am afraid my son will have another seizure. Because: The kids will see it and that is not a good thing, and I don't know that I can handle another one. Because: I don't want my son to die. Bingo! That was the real reason I was scared. Admitting it was my first big step.

I made the choice to state my wants: I wanted my son to do exactly what the doctor said to avoid future seizures.

I had to dig deeper. By following doctor's orders and not having any more seizures, what would that accomplish for me? What do I really want? To not feel scared anymore. To not tell stories about my son's death in my head. To not see doomsday every time I look at him. To own my potency and stop feeling sorry for myself.

I moved to Resourceful: What strategies will I use to get what I want? I will focus on the glass half full. I will appreciate what I learned about his condition so I can be more equipped to help when / if it happens again. I will relish the times we are together, have fun, connect with him in the way that is healthy. I will take care of myself; attend to my psychological needs so as not to drain my bucket. I will ask for hugs and share my feelings often.

Then I made the choice to let go, move on, and make some commitments to myself: How will I see these new strategies through? Lots of self talk and self reflection. I will stop the negative voice in my head and realize this is just a "script" and that this habitual pattern can be changed. Stay away from projecting the Myth, "You can make me feel bad if you don't take your medications." Start the minute I step out of the bathtub.

How will I know these strategies are working? Pay attention to ME, check and adjust. Look for additional strategies that are helpful.

Finally, I made the choice to stop and listen, returning to Open.

When I finished this cycle, I cried. A lot. And my cry was different. I didn't cry out of desperation because I didn't know what to do, or how to move on, or how to deal with the reality of this condition. I cried because I was sad, and that was OK. I cried because I felt relieved for taking control over what I can, for knowing how to move on, and for being able to let go of things I can't control.

Did I find myself in the dumps again for the same reason? YES. Did I have to review/revisit these questions to "adjust" myself periodically? Absolutely. This takes work. I am still working at it. And, it is getting easier every day. I am grateful for the structure and guidance I received from The Formula that day. It helped me get through a very difficult time, and it helps me deal with stress and conflict every day.

MATURITY IS LIVING A MYTHLESS LIFE

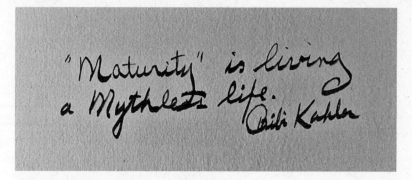

At our headquarters in Newton, KS we encourage people to write on our walls. This picture is a quote by one of my mentors, Taibi Kahler. The quote captures the essence of compassionate accountability. When we struggle with others in positive conflict to create something amazing, we reject the myths that we can make anyone feel good or bad emotionally, or that they could do the same to us. A mythless life allows conflict without casualties because we think, feel, and act as though people (including ourselves) are worthwhile, capable, and accountable.

It is my sincere wish that you have found affirmation in this book, are inspired with new skills and ideas, and are ready to make new commitments for how you engage in conflict. I request that you join me, my team at Next Element, our worldwide network of facilitators, practitioners and providers, our growing number of clients, and our family and friends who are working to end the energy crisis of drama. Whatever your scope of influence, you have the ability to spread compassionate accountability and change the world.

Conflict without casualties can become a reality in your life.

- Use the Personal Development Guide in Appendix A to enhance your learning experience.

Appendix A

PERSONAL DEVELOPMENT GUIDE

If you would like to dive a little deeper into the concepts from each chapter, this section will help you. Geared specifically for those on a journey of personal discovery and growth, the items in this section will help you challenge yourself towards greater levels of awareness and effectiveness. If you are involved in a coaching or counseling relationship, this section will be an invaluable resource for your work. I recommend documenting your work in a journal so you can keep track of your progress and reflect back on the journey.

INTEGRATING YOUR DRAMA-RESILIENCE ASSESSMENT (DRA™) RESULTS

Any great learning quest involves a solid assessment of your current state, and measurement of change along the way. We've developed the Drama Resilience Assessment (DRA™), an online tool, to gain insight into your drama tendencies and compassion potentials. Go to www.next-element.com/conflict-without-casualties to complete one free assessment and receive your basic DRA™ report. Use these results along with this personal development guide to enhance the impact of the book.

If you are working with a Leading Out of Drama (LOD®) certified professional he/she may help you get your DRA™ report. A comprehensive DRA™ report that includes seven key indexes of drama and compassion is available only through certified LOD® practitioner or provider. Visit next-element.com to learn more.

Do you want to measure change in your compassionate accountability? Take the DRA™ again after you've completed the book or at periodic intervals during your coaching relationship and compare your results.

CHAPTER 1
Conflict: The Big Bang of Communication

- What is your relationship with conflict? How have you experienced it in the past?
- Who were your role-models for conflict growing up? How has that shaped how you handle conflict?
- Compassion is about struggling with others instead of against them. How does this fit with your understanding of compassion?
- Describe some of your heroes who demonstrate compassion. What do you admire about them?
- Why are you reading this book? What would you like to get out of it? What broad goals would you like set?

CHAPTER 2
Drama: Misusing the Energy of Conflict

If you have taken a DRA™, your report will have a risk index for each of the three Drama Roles. The closer your score is to 100, the more frequently you will play this role. If you don't have a report, you can combine what you know about yourself with what you've learned in this chapter to make your best guess.

- What feelings did you experience at different points when reading this chapter? What might they be telling you?
- What drama roles do you customarily play? Review your DRA™ results and compare this to how you view yourself. Is it accurate? What discrepancies do you see?
- Think of a particular drama situation in your life. What roles did the different parties play? What role(s) did you play?
- Review the section titled *Cultural Consequences of Drama-Based Leadership*. Then consider: Is your drama behavior contributing to any negative cultural consequences?
- What connections do you see between your drama behaviors and your strengths?

- What does drama cost you personally and professionally? Consider the emotional, psychological, social, physical and spiritual consequences.
- What insights and connections have you made about drama in your life? List several key learnings.
- What changes would you like to make in your own behaviors as a leader, parent, friend, peer, coach, or other type of change agent?
- What decisions or commitments will you make going forward?
- What support or resources would help you most in making these changes? How will you begin to access those resources?

CHAPTER 3
But I'm Just Trying to Help!:
Good Intentions, Unintended Consequences

Your Drama-Based Helping Patterns and most likely Drama Allies and Adversaries are part of the comprehensive DRA™ profile report. If your report doesn't include these results or if you haven't completed your report, you can combine what you know about yourself with what you've learned in this chapter to make your best guess about your most likely drama allies and adversaries.

- While reading this chapter, what feelings did you experience at different points? What might they be telling you?
- What type of drama-based helping pattern is most common for you? What feelings, thoughts, and behaviors let you know that you're trying to help from a drama role?
- What insights or connections did you make about drama-based helping in your life? List several key learnings.
- Who are your Drama Allies? Do you participate in any of the gossip described in this chapter? What have been the personal and professional consequences?
- Who are your Drama Adversaries? Do you get caught up in habitual patterns of interaction that end in the same unsatisfying way every time?
- What insights or connections did you make about drama allies and adversaries in your life? List several key learnings.
- What changes would you like to make in your own behaviors as a leader, parent, friend, peer, coach, or other type of change agent?
- What decisions or commitments will you make going forward?

- What support or resources would help you most in making these changes? How will you begin to access those resources?

CHAPTER 4
Compassion: Not for the Faint of Heart

If you have taken a DRA™, your strength in each of the three Compassion Skills will be shown on your profile report. The closer your score is to 100, the stronger this skill is for you. If you don't have a report, you can combine what you know about yourself with what you've learned in this chapter to make your best guess.

- While reading this chapter, what emotions did you experience at different points? What might they be telling you?
- What are your compassion strengths? What are your weaknesses? Review the three strategies for each compassion skill and rank them in order of strongest to weakest for you. Where do you see these strengths and challenges playing out in your life?
- Where in your life have you used compassion skills to combat drama invitations? What has worked for you? What can you build on?
- What is the balance among your compassion skills? Is one more or less developed than the others? What implications does this have for how you deal with drama?
- What insights or connections did you make about compassion skills in your life? List several key learnings.
- What changes would you like to make in your own behaviors as a leader, parent, friend, peer, coach, or other type of change agent?
- What decisions or commitments will you make going forward?
- What support or resources would help you most in making these changes? How will you begin to access those resources?

CHAPTER 5
Compassion and the Cycles of Human Civilization: Will We Get It Right This Time?

This chapter does not have a corresponding DRA™ index.

- How did you experience this chapter in the context of what you've read so far?

- What is your perspective on Braden's revised view of our past as humans, compared to traditional thinking on the topic? How does it challenge any beliefs you have about how humans have developed on earth?
- In this chapter, I suggest that humans struggle with moving from Persistence back to Openness and that this causes a lot of our problems. Do you agree? Disagree? Why? What is your experience?
- Where do you personally struggle to stay on the Compassion Cycle? What drama invitations are most tempting for you?
- What insights or connections did you make about yourself during this chapter?
- What changes would you like to make in your own behaviors as a leader, parent, friend, peer, coach, or other type of change agent?
- What decisions or commitments will you make going forward?
- What support or resources would help you most in making these changes? How will you begin to access those resources?

CHAPTER 6
Violators Will be Prosecuted: Three Rules of the Compassion Cycle
This chapter does not have a corresponding DRA™ index.

- While reading this chapter, what emotions did you experience at different points? What might they be telling you?
- If you were in Sally's position, how would you feel about the response she got from Juanita at the coffee shop? Have you ever experienced someone refusing to accept your drama invitations? How did you feel?
- The first rule of the Compassion Cycle is to start at open. How easy or difficult is this for you? Why?
- Reflect on the paradox of openness being both vulnerable and strong. What's your perspective? What about this challenges you?
- This chapter has a table of the most likely consequences of skipping each skill on the Compassion Cycle. Which one(s) relate to you the most? Why?
- What insights or connections did you make about yourself during this chapter?
- What changes would you like to make in your own behaviors as a leader, parent, friend, peer, coach, or other type of change agent?
- What decisions or commitments will you make going forward?

- What support or resources would help you most in making these changes? How will you begin to access those resources?

CHAPTER 7
Warning! Drama Approaching!: Three Leading Indicators

If you have completed the DRA™ full report, your profile will show your risk index for each of the three Leading Indicators. If you do not have the full report, you can combine what you know about yourself with what you've learned in this chapter to make your best guess.

- What emotions did you experience while you were reading this chapter? What might they be telling you?
- Which Leading Indicator(s) are most prevalent for you? How do they show themselves in your life? What are the consequences?
- Each Leading Indicator is followed by three personal affirmations to help you get back on track. Which ones resonated most with you? Which ones do you think are most important for you to accept? Which ones will be easiest and most difficult?
- What insights or connections did you make about yourself during this chapter?
- What changes would you like to make in your own behaviors as a leader, parent, friend, peer, coach, or other type of change agent?
- What decisions or commitments will you make going forward?
- What support or resources would help you most in making these changes? How will you begin to access those resources?

CHAPTER 8
It's All About Choices: Three Choices to Move

If you have completed the DRA™ full report, your profile report will show your three Choices to Move competency scores: State Your Wants, Let Go and Move On, and Stop and Listen. Use these, in conjunction with your own experience, to explore your ability to make the three Choices to Move and set goals for personal growth. If you do not have the full report, use your best guess as to your strength in each Choice to Move.

- What emotions did you experience while you were reading this chapter? What might they be telling you?

- How do you feel about identifying and sharing your feelings and intentions with others? What barriers do you erect?
- Which of the three Choices to Move is easiest for you to make? Which is most difficult? Why?
- Letting Go and Moving On involves a series of losses outlined in this chapter. Which losses resonate most with you? Why?
- In the case study, *Dan: The CEO Who Couldn't Let Go and Move On*, what resonated most with you? Do you see characteristics of yourself in Dan? What are they?
- Are you stuck at Persistence and unable to stop and listen? What is your heart, body, and soul telling you?
- Practice the exercise outlined in the section; *Stop and Listen: Make the Choice to Practice Empathy.* What did you experience?
- What insights or connections did you make about yourself during this chapter?
- What changes would you like to make in your own behaviors as a result of what you read in this chapter?
- What decisions or commitments will you make going forward?
- What support or resources would help you most in making these changes? How will you begin to access those resources?

CHAPTER 9
Coaching Accountability When There's No Drama: Match and Move
This chapter does not have a corresponding DRA™ index.

- What emotions did you experience while you were reading this chapter? What might they be telling you?
- What experiences have you had with helpers in your life who either met you where you were at, or expected you to join them at their level?
- For each Compassion Skill, there are additional phrases to Match and Move. Do any of these resonate with you? Why?
- Match and Move works up, down, or sideways. Which one would be easiest for you? Most challenging?
- What insights or connections did you make about yourself during this chapter?
- What changes would you like to make in your own behaviors as a leader, parent, friend, peer, coach, or other type of change agent?

- What decisions or commitments will you make going forward?
- What support or resources would help you most in making these changes? How will you begin to access those resources?

CHAPTER 10
The Formula for Compassionate Conflict:
Confronting Drama with Compassionate Accountability
This chapter does not have a corresponding DRA™ index.

- What emotions did you experience while you were reading this chapter? What might they be telling you?
- Write down your own ORPO statement to address a conflict in your life. Say it to yourself, then share it with a trusted peer, friend, coach, or mentor. Get feedback and adjust if needed.•
- Practice using the template for an ORPO apology to apologize to someone in your life. How did it go? What did you experience? What did you learn?
- The chapter ends with tips for ORPO success. Which ones will be easiest for you? Most challenging? Why?
- What insights or connections did you make about yourself during this chapter?
- What changes would you like to make in your own behaviors as a leader, parent, friend, peer, coach, or other type of change agent?
- What decisions or commitments will you make going forward?
- What support or resources would help you most in making these changes? How will you begin to access those resources?

CHAPTER 11
Conflict without Casualties: Preparing to Struggle with
This chapter does not have a corresponding DRA™ index.

- What emotions did you experience while you were reading this chapter? What might they be telling you?
- Reflect on the two stress-coping habits. Which one is more likely for you? How does it show itself in your life?
- Stress has a lot to do with perception. What perceptions do you have about conflict that increase your stress?

- Four stress-coping habits are described in this chapter. In which one(s) are you most likely to engage? What are the consequences?
- Practice building your ORPO bank by using the template in Appendix B. Make copies of the template and work through the seven steps for a couple different conflict situations in your life. Share and debrief this with your coach, mentor, trusted friend, or peer.
- This chapter describes six emotional motives that lurk behind most drama. Which one(s) resonate most with you? Why?
- What insights or connections did you make about yourself during this chapter?
- What changes would you like to make in your own behaviors as a leader, parent, friend, peer, coach, or other type of change agent?
- What decisions or commitments will you make going forward?
- What support or resources would help you most in making these changes? How will you begin to access those resources?

Appendix B

PREPARING FOR CONFLICT:

BUILDING MY ORPO BANK

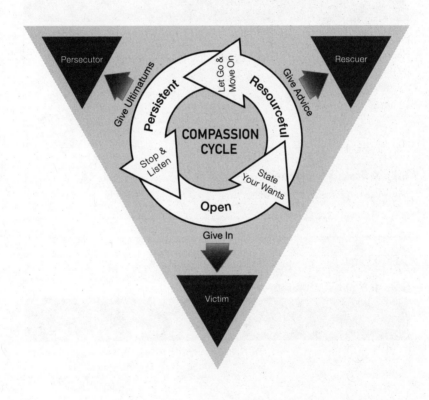

Make copies of this template to use for each new situation. Use what you write to apply the Formula for Compassionate Conflict and ORPO statements.

Step 1: Mind the Gap

The situation I want to address is:

_____

_____

_____

Step 2: Build Your Open Bank

How I can empathize through past experience:	Feelings the other person(s) might have and how I will validate them:	Feelings I'm willing to disclose are:

Step 3: State Your Wants

My emotional motives and wants are:

_____

_____

_____

Step 4: Build Your Resourceful Bank

Relevant resources to gather or share are:	Past successes I could build on are:	Personal strengths I could leverage are:

Step 5: Choose to Let Go and Move on

In order to move on, I will have to let go of:

_____

_____

_____

Step 6: Build your Persistence Bank

My boundaries and commitments are:	Non-negotiables I want to reinforce are:	I am willing to accept responsibility for:

Step 7: Stop and Listen

How am I feeling about engaging in conflict this way? How are others involved in the conflict feeling about it?

_____

_____

_____

Notes

Notes

Chapter 2

1   Regier, N. & King, J. (2013). *Beyond Drama: Transcending Energy Vampires*. Next Element Press, Newton, KS
2   Kahler, T. (2008). The Process Therapy Model: Six Personality Types with Adaptations. Taibi Kahler Associates, Inc.
3   When my colleagues in France teach the Drama Triangle, they use the French term "savior" to reinforce the "god-like" attitude and willingness to be a martyr.
4   David Kaiser, CEO of H2H Dynamics. Research based on a poll of 600 organizational leaders.
5   CPP Inc., publishers of the Myers-Briggs Assessment and the Thomas-Kilmann Conflict Mode Instrument— commissioned a study on workplace conflict, 2008. Get the full report at http://img.en25.com/Web/CPP/ Conflict_report.pdf
6   We are fans of the Process Communication Model (PCM®), a behavioral communication model of individual differences, discovered but Dr. Taibi Kahler, that shows how positive and negative attention behaviors are related to different personality types. We've used the PCM® listing of positive character strengths, with some variation, as our point of reference.
7   https://hbr.org/2015/12/its-better-to-avoid-a-toxic-employee-than-hire-a-superstar
8   http://www.careerbuilder.com/share/aboutus/pressreleasesdetail.aspx?sd=12/13/2012&id=pr730&ed=12/31/2012

Chapter 3

1   In the Process Communication Model, Dr. Kahler's discovery of First Degree Drivers demonstrated predictable and subtle changes in words, tones, gestures, postures, and facial expressions that occur when thinking gets contaminated by myths, inviting negative responses from others.

Chapter 4

1   Arbinger Institute (2010). *Leadership and Self-Deception: Getting Out of the Box*. Arbinger Institute.
2   https://hbr.org/2015/05/why-compassion-is-a-better-managerial-tactic-than-toughness
3   Many people have adapted or modified Karpman's original work, without his permission or endorsement, to develop their own leadership and conflict models. Our methodology evolved and is being used with Karpman's permission and support.
4   http://www.sethgodin.com/
5   https://en.wikipedia.org/wiki/Mirror_neuron
6   http://ideas.ted.com/the-secret-ingredient-that-makes-some-teams-better-than-others/
7   http://www.6seconds.org/2015/08/06/precious-feelings-or-maxs-nap/
8   http://brenebrown.com/
9   Talgam, Itay. *The Ignorant Maestro: How Great Leaders Inspire Unpredictable Brilliance*. Penguin Random House, New York. http://www.talgam.com/book
10 All about Curiosity - blog by Leadership Freak https://leadershipfreak.wordpress.com/2015/09/02/21952/
11 Maxwell, J. (2000). *Failing Forward: Turning Mistakes into Stepping Stones for Success*. Thomas-Nelson Publishers.

12 https://hbr.org/2015/08/amazon-is-right-that-disagreement-results-in-better-decisions
13 Lencioni, P. (2002). *The Five Dysfunctions of a Team: A Leadership Fable*. Josses-Bass, San Francisco.
14 Duckworth, A. (2016). *Grit: The Power of Passion and Perseverance*. Scribner, New York.
15 A phrase referring to a person who is noteworthy for only a single achievement, skill, or characteristic. The phrase originated with a performing animal (especially a pony) that knows only one trick.

Chapter 5

1 Braden, G. (2011). *Deep Truth: Igniting the Memory of Our Origin, History, Destiny, and Fate*. Hay House, Inc., New York.
2 Stephen Karpman argues that even at a cellular level, the three compassion skills are played by various parts of a healthy cell. One set of cells provides a Resupply of chemicals and hormones (Resourceful) to the awaiting Reception cells (Open), while a third set of Restriction cells manages the resupply rates to ensure homeostasis (Persistent). Illness can result from a malfunction of any or all of these roles. For example, autoimmune diseases occur when Restriction cells become Persecutors. http://www.karpmandramatriangle.com/pdf/thenewdrama-triangles.pdf
3 The trio of feelings, thoughts, and actions is a common theme in psychosocial theory and research. For example, Albert Bandura's self-efficacy theory postulates that human experience is made up of affective (feelings), cognitive (thoughts), and behavioral (actions) components.
4 Some examples include: Evolution (biological change in organisms), Beck's Change Model (change in human systems), Spiral Dynamics Integral (change in value memes), and Plan Do, Check Act (PDCA Cycle) in change management.

Chapter 7

1 https://en.wikipedia.org/wiki/Go_ahead,_make_my_day
2 I later learned about my personality structure through the lens of the Process Communication Model. I finally understood the natural power struggles between different personalities and how these struggles can be eliminated when people are motivated according to their own psychological needs. A personal mission of mine is to help leaders guide talented but wayward apprentices to find their path with less collateral damage. Conflict without casualties.

Chapter 8

1 Victimization is different from playing the Victim role. I've done a lot of work with victims of domestic violence who are making very calculated decisions each day to control what they can and stay safe. I don't advocate using any of the strategies in this book if you are in imminent physical danger or dealing with a person who is intent on causing physical harm and seems to have no conscience. However, these strategies have proven to be extremely helpful in working with victimized persons who are trying to rebuild their self-esteem and learn new habits for communication and relationships.

Chapter 9

1 Mirroring is a rapport-building technique that involves behavior that "mirrors" the other person. The intention is to show alignment in both words and body language. Active listening is a strategy that involves restating what was heard with the goal of developing and showing authentic understanding of the speaker's feelings, needs, and ideas.
2 The Process Communication Model (PCM®) is an extremely effective language-based behavioral model for motivating different personality types. It is a terrific complement to the positive conflict and accountability methods described in this book. This is why it's a staple of our leadership, coaching, and train the trainer programs.

Chapter 11

1 The Process Communication Model (PCM®) and The Birkman Method are the best, in my opinion, because they offer specific guidelines on what motivates you and how you can get these needs met in a healthy way every day. Next Element specializes in PCM.®

Glossary of Terms and Phrases

Compassion
Compassion is what happens when we struggle with others and ourselves, with intention, to be effective and take responsibility for our behaviors and choices, in order to create something amazing.

Compassion Cycle
Next Element's model for "struggling *with*" self and others by engaging in positive conflict through compassionate accountability.

Compassionate Accountability
The process of engaging in positive conflict for the purpose of catalyzing positive outcomes.

Drama
Drama is what happens when we struggle against ourselves or each other, with or without awareness, to feel justified about our negative behavior.

Drama Adversary
Someone who reinforces your drama position by playing a complementary drama role. The motive is to pit two roles against each other.

Drama Ally
Someone who reinforces your drama position by helping you justify your drama role. The motive is to join roles against a third party.

Drama-Based Helping
Helping while in a drama role. Good intentions often result in unintended negative consequences

Drama Resilience Assessment
Next Element's online assessment of a person's drama risks and compassion potential.

Formula for Compassionate Conflict
The strategy for responding to drama with positive conflict. It is known as O-R-P-O, which stands for Openness, Resourcefulness, Persistence, and Openness.

Karpman's Drama Triangle
A diagram developed by Dr. Stephen Karpman showing the unhealthy dynamics played between the roles of Victim, Persecutor, and Rescuer in the throes of drama.

Match and Move
The technique for facilitating compassionate accountability when there is no drama. Match the compassion skill, then invite the appropriate choice to move.

Openness
The healthy alternative to Victim, involving transparency, courage with self and others, self-awareness, empathy, confidence in one's own adequacy, and a willingness to ask for and receive help.

Persecutor
A drama role that verbally attacks or blames from a position of "I'm OK. You're NOT OK."

Persistence
The healthy alternative to Persecuting. It involves dependability, perseverance, courage, enforcing boundaries in healthy ways and a commitment to optimism.

Rescuer

A drama role that overdoes for someone, reinforcing overdependence from a position of "I'm OK. You're OK if you accept my help."

Resourcefulness

The healthy alternative to Rescuing. It involves creativity, openmindedness, curiosity, problem-solving, innovation, the quest for discovery, and the resilience to bounce back from failure.

Three Choices to Move

Three key decisions for personal responsibility that must be made in order for a person to move around the Compassion Cycle and adhere to the Three Rules.

Three Rules of the Compassion Cycle

Rules that govern the best use of compassion skills to engage in positive conflict.

Three Leading Indicators for Drama

Warning signs that a person is slipping into drama.

Victim

A drama role that over-adapts or feels hurt in response to being attacked or blamed, from a position of "I'm NOT OK. You're OK."

Index

About the Author

I am the CEO and co-founding owner of Next Element Consulting, a global leadership advisory group. We started this journey in 2008 with a vision for training, coaching, and certifying change-agents to communicate better, especially during conflict. Next Element supports a growing network of trainers, coaches, and advisors around the world who share our passion for "struggling with" others and want to make a difference in their communities, organizations, and families.

Nate Regier.
Gavin Peters Photography

We are also parents with friends and colleagues and messy extended families. We know the heartbreak and failures and bitter costs of poor communication. We challenge ourselves each day to put into practice what we teach. We challenge ourselves each day to put into practice what we teach. Our company is a dynamic laboratory for testing, refining, and applying the tools we share with others. Our goal is to increase positive energy in the world, one person at a time, starting with ourselves.

We've trained with, climbed with, and have been guided by some of the most influential communicators in the world. We are pioneering the art and science of applying compassionate accountability to improve relationships and business results. Visit next-element.com to learn more.

While we are deeply committed to solid theory and research, it is behavior change that ultimately matters. When people communicate differently with each other, trust can happen, productivity can happen, great cultures can happen.

Building cultures of compassionate accountability.
(316) 283-4200   next-element.com

How Drama Resilient Are You?

Every journey starts with an accurate assessment of where you are. Free with this book is your opportunity to take Next Element's Drama Resilience Assessment (DRA)® to measure your drama risks and compassion potentials. Follow these simple steps:

1. Go to www.next-element.com/conflict-without-casualties
2. Click on the Claim Free Assessment button
3. Click on the Take Your DRA button
4. Answer a few secret questions, and click the Submit and Take the Assessment button
5. Complete the DRA and get your results.

Use your DRA to add context and clarity to your personal journey, book study, team-building, or coaching work. Each chapter in the book refers to portions of the DRA, and Appendix A offers even more ways to explore and apply what you are learning.

Start building your culture of compassionate accountability today!

Berrett–Koehler
Publishers

Berrett-Koehler is an independent publisher dedicated to an ambitious mission: Connecting people and ideas to create a world that works for all.

We believe that the solutions to the world's problems will come from all of us, working at all levels: in our organizations, in our society, and in our own lives. Our BK Business books help people make their organizations more humane, democratic, diverse, and effective (we don't think there's any contradiction there). Our BK Currents books offer pathways to creating a more just, equitable, and sustainable society. Our BK Life books help people create positive change in their lives and align their personal practices with their aspirations for a better world.

All of our books are designed to bring people seeking positive change together around the ideas that empower them to see and shape the world in a new way.

And we strive to practice what we preach. At the core of our approach is Stewardship, a deep sense of responsibility to administer the company for the benefit of all of our stakeholder groups including authors, customers, employees, investors, service providers, and the communities and environment around us. Everything we do is built around this and our other key values of quality, partnership, inclusion, and sustainability.

This is why we are both a B-Corporation and a California Benefit Corporation—a certification and a for-profit legal status that require us to adhere to the highest standards for corporate, social, and environmental performance.

We are grateful to our readers, authors, and other friends of the company who consider themselves to be part of the BK Community. We hope that you, too, will join us in our mission.

A BK Business Book

We hope you enjoy this BK Business book. BK Business books pioneer new leadership and management practices and socially responsible approaches to business. They are designed to provide you with groundbreaking and practical tools to transform your work and organizations while upholding the triple bottom line of people, planet, and profits. High-five!

To find out more, visit **www.bkconnection.com**.

Berrett–Koehler
Publishers

Connecting people and ideas
to create a world that works for all

Dear Reader,

Thank you for picking up this book and joining our worldwide community of Berrett-Koehler readers. We share ideas that bring positive change into people's lives, organizations, and society.

To welcome you, we'd like to offer you a free e-book. You can pick from among twelve of our bestselling books by entering the promotional code **BKP92E** here: http://www.bkconnection.com/welcome.

When you claim your free e-book, we'll also send you a copy of our e-newsletter, the *BK Communiqué*. Although you're free to unsubscribe, there are many benefits to sticking around. In every issue of our newsletter you'll find

• A free e-book
• Tips from famous authors
• Discounts on spotlight titles
• Hilarious insider publishing news
• A chance to win a prize for answering a riddle

Best of all, our readers tell us, "Your newsletter is the only one I actually read." So claim your gift today, and please stay in touch!

Sincerely,

Charlotte Ashlock
Steward of the BK Website

Questions? Comments? Contact me at bkcommunity@bkpub.com.

MIX
Paper from
responsible sources
FSC® C016245
www.fsc.org

Certified
Corporation
bcorporation.net